Birthing
into
Spirit

The Journey of the Soul
continues after Physical Death

KATYE ANNA

BIRTHING INTO SPIRIT
The Journey of the Soul continues after Physical Death

Published by:
Transformation Books
211 Pauline Drive #513
York, PA 17402
www.TransformationBooks.com

ISBN: 978-0-9851407-9-3

Printed in the United States of America

A portion of the proceeds from the sale of this book will be donated to the charities the author supports.

Birthing
into
Spirit

The Journey of the Soul
continues after Physical Death

NOTES TO THE READER

When I wrote my first book *"Into the Light"* I did not realize it at the time but writing the stories and sharing the journeys of those birthing into spirit was my way of working through my grief. I was not ready to deal with the issues I now write about in *"Birthing into Spirit"*.

The information for both books poured in as a steady stream of consciousness from my soul. Both books had a life of their own. I share the same stories in both books but in *"Birthing into Spirit"* I share about death with dignity and outline my vision for the future as we educate people about birthing into spirit. The stories are true. The names Sam and Lana have been changed. I have been blessed to be with people as they birth back into spirit. They have each taught me important life lessons. There is a lot we can learn from those who are birthing into spirit. They have also helped me to step up and begin teaching that how we die is as important as how we live.

DEDICATION

I dedicate this book to the souls known as David Mummert, Debbie Krause and my beloved soul companion John Guy Baublitz III. I also dedicate this book to the many souls who have taught me as well as loved me.

I want to thank my husband Allan for his love and encouragement. I thank my mother Kathryn Mummert for encouraging me to be different through the many twists and turns of our lives together as mother and daughter. I thank my beautiful children and grandchildren for their love, encouragement and support. I thank my teachers of light for their support and guidance throughout my life. I am humbled by their daily presence in my life.

To Christine Kloser I want to say, "Thank you" for her encouragement and support. She has been a wealth of information and has offered her support in getting my books published.

CONTENTS

CHAPTER ONE

BIRTHING INTO SPIRIT IS A JOURNEY WE WILL ALL TAKE

There comes a time in everyone's journey when life on earth comes to an end. The sacred journey of the incarnated soul which began at birth begins to move its energy and consciousness toward birthing onto spirit. The subject of death is one most people will avoid until they are forced to deal with it. How one embraces birthing into spirit is often determined by how one has lived their life. One of our goals is to have the experience of dying, birthing into spirit, be an experience that people are comfortable talking about and begin to embrace as a part of the journey of the soul.

Many families find it hard to talk about life talking about death is difficult if not impossible. This book is written to give people hope, encouragement and a new way to think about life and death. Embracing that we are incarnated souls gives new meaning to life. Being incarnated souls, the dying process need not be feared but embraced as a part of the journey of the soul.

When a child is born others are there to support the process. The needs of the mother and child are watched over carefully by those in attendance. At any time if mother or child is in distress there is help. Midwives are trained, as are those supporting the mother, to help encourage the mother through the process of childbirth. Birthing into spirit offers the same support and care for the dying process.

Imagine a world where dying is embraced as a part of the journey of the incarnated soul. Death is not seen as an ending but a continuation of the journey. Birthing into spirit coaches will be trained in the future to support the process of those who are leaving the physical life and returning to spirit. As in childbirth when the physical body is in distress help is there to ensure that the birthing into spirit process honors and helps the incarnated soul leaves the physical body with grace.

Much work has been done by hospice workers all over the world to give comfort care to those who are dying. Birthing into spirit includes care for the incarnated soul whose physical life is ending. Honoring that we are incarnated souls begins to bring into one's life and experiences that the journey of the soul is one which continues after physical death, thus the term birthing into spirit. Birthing into spirit coaches honor the personal and religious beliefs of the person whose physical journey is ending. Birthing into spirit coaches help the family, medical staff and the one birthing into spirit communicate about all aspects of emotional, spiritual and physical care, including the right to die with grace.

We are excited when a child is born. In chapter five I share how David made a conscious choice to die. During his birthing into spirit process he shared that if we could see where he was going we would all be excited for him. The excitement and anticipation felt with the birth of a child can be experienced by those birthing into spirit. David wanted his family to understand how beautiful it was where he was going. He was ready to leave the physical body which no longer allowed him to do the things he loved. He told us that no one is really ever ready to let go of those they have loved during life but let go we all must do.

David understood that although he was leaving those he loved who still experienced life, thus consciousness on earth, he was returning home to the world of spirit. He knew he would have a grand reunion with those who had birthed into spirit before him. David's message of hope, of a beautiful place and loved ones who exists in this place he called heaven gives hope that something awaits us as we let go of the physical body.

Letting go of loved ones, relationships, and the physical body is not easy even when one understands that consciousness continues after physical life. The challenge for those birthing into spirit is about letting go of the physical. Birthing into spirit coaches are trained in the process of creating space for those who are birthing into spirit to talk about what they are feeling and seeing.

Perhaps for the first time in their life personalities are encouraged to share their feelings. The process of birthing into spirit offers a pathway for everyone to embrace healing as the personality moves through stages of birthing into spirit. Conversations with loved ones are encouraged. Birthing into spirit coaches hold space and encourage the expansion of spiritual consciousness as one lets go of physical consciousness.

The stories shared in this book are stories of love. Each person experienced the journey of birthing into spirit differently. Magali shares in her story that those who were focusing on her physical body when she birthed into spirit, could not see that she was still in the room, no longer physical but beautiful and free in her body of light.

I had a brother tell me recently he wasn't into death the way I am. Truth is my life's work has been about life and helping people embrace that we are incarnated souls. My life's work has focused on helping people live consciously so they can die consciously. The focus of my work has been to help people touch that part of them that is spirit. Writing this book and offering teachings, which help people, embrace physical death as a part of the journey of the soul is part of my soul's life plan.

Birthing into spirit isn't a catch phase I use. I believe that we are spiritual beings. We incarnate into this world for the purpose of soul growth and soul expansion. When we die a physical death, the spark of our soul which inhabited the body continues experiencing consciousness, thus the term birthing into spirit.

In our book "Conscious Construction of the Soul" Anna teaches that when a child is born we should honor that this infant child is God individualized through physical birth.

An excerpt from "Conscious Construction of the Soul":

"Honor the creative force of soul which has now merged with the physical. And then honor the creative force of soul which dwells within you. Remember that within you is the spark of creator God. All of those in attendance at a child's birth have just witnessed the miracle of spirit and flesh becoming united.

We remind you of the composition of the incarnated soul. At the severing of the cord the soul sends forth the living spark of soul essence into the body of the newborn and with it its energy bodies of light begin to take shape and form. With each physical breath the light bodies and the physical form begin to give birth to the spiritual manifestation of the soul.

The soul has created a physical form in which it will navigate the physical plane of reality. Once the union of physical and spirit have merged the birthing process is complete. Life of the spiritual being begins with the severing of the cord. Once dependent on the mother for each breath the child now begins to breathe on its own and with each breath grounds into the physical the essence of the soul which will experience life."

What would our lives and our experiences about death be like if we honored that the creative force of soul continues to experience consciousness after physical death? When one's physical life begins to come to an end that which has been made manifest, the physical and spirit, now begin the journey of birthing into spirit. The vehicle, the physical body, has served its grand purpose and now spirit and physical must begin the letting go process.

The process of life is very much like the process of death. We spend our entire lives learning how to let go. We are challenged everyday to expand our consciousness and to let go of old outdated believes, wounds, and patterns which prevent us from fully embracing the magnificence of our souls. The way we deal with letting go of relationships, experiences wounds of the past during our life determines how we will let go when physical death approaches.

Those birthing into spirit begin the journey of letting go of the physical. What childbirth was to the incarnating soul is now the dance of one birthing into spirit. Childbirth used to be a sacred dance between mother, child and the incarnating soul. The sacredness of childbirth has been forgotten by the masses as has the sacredness of dying a physical death.

Most personalities have no understanding that they are incarnated souls and within them is the spark of Creator God. They see themselves as purely physical. They live their lives focused on physical consciousness. For many it is not until dying that personalities allow themselves to see through spiritual consciousness. The veil has been removed. Seeing beings of light, departed loved ones, and moving freely between planes of consciousness becomes a part of the birthing into spirit journey.

Birthing into spirit is a sacred and conscious process of honoring that the physical life and time on Mother Earth is ending. Birthing into spirit also honors that although the physical body is shutting down, consciousness maintained in the light body returns to soul.

We spend our entire lives trying to bring more soul essence into our life. For many this is an unconscious process. Everyone has their own way of experiencing the divine. In chapter six I share the journey of Johnny as he birthed into spirit. During his last ten days on earth he told us that we all had God within us and we each had to decide how much of God we want others to see. Awakening to the truth that we are incarnated souls and the journey of the soul is on-going can be liberating and can occur in one's life long before one births into spirit. Bringing forth the divine spark of God and allowing others to see our light is a part of the journey of the soul.

Many personalities believe there is a heaven, a place loved ones go and wait for us to join them. Interestingly enough most people when asked believe that heaven is only a place that good people go to. In truth the concept of heaven isn't understood. Pearly gates and life everlasting with a religious God are concepts many have of heaven. Heaven is not a "place" that is the same for everyone, nor is "heaven" a place only good people go to. Believing they will someday be reunited with their loved ones offers people hope. Hope is a beautiful gift as is the belief that our loved ones are in heaven.

The gift of birthing into spirit if embraced, teaches us that we don't have to wait until someday to be reunited with our loved ones. When we can begin to embrace the magnificence of the journey of our souls we will begin to understand that death does not separate us from those who have birth into spirit. What separates us is our focus on physical consciousness. Within Creator God there can be no separation.

Birthing into spirit seeks to help shift consciousness, for those who are ready. This consciousness shift requires us to embrace that we are incarnated souls. By embracing that we are incarnated souls we can begin to hold space for those who are dying a physical death because physical death is a part of the journey of the soul. Doing so allows us to understand that physical death only occurs to the body. The journey of the soul continues and consciousness of the personality returns to the soul.

CHAPTER TWO

EMBRACING SPIRITUAL CONSCIOUSNESS

We are each on a journey of the soul and we each have within us the creative spark of God. For the most part personalities have forgotten that they have within them the creative spark of God. This creative spark is ours no matter what the journey, no matter what the beliefs of the tribe, no matter where one's choices have taken them on this journey. The journey of the incarnated soul takes each of our lives through many twists and turns of life ending with physical death. Through the lens of physical consciousness we view our lives as limited and we view death as something to fear.

Within each one of us is the power to move beyond the world of physical consciousness into the world of spirit consciousness. There are clear distinctions between the two worlds.

Physical consciousness creates experiences of fear versus love. Physical consciousness tells us that death is something to fear. Physical consciousness tells us death is the end of life. Physical consciousness tells us that what we see, hear, taste, touch and smell is what's real. Physical consciousness tells us that someday after we die we will go to heaven and be with our loved one.

Spiritual consciousness tells us that death is a part of the journey of the incarnated soul. Spiritual consciousness tells us that with the death of the physical body consciousness continues and returns to this place many call heaven. Spiritual consciousness opens our experiences to include the world of spirit.

Most personalities continue to create experiences based on beliefs of the tribe. The stories of a loved one dying a slow death alone in their room have been imprinted in us all. Fear associated with not only dying but how we die pushes thinking, much less talking, about death into the shadows of our consciousness. Sadness and despair over what we imprint as a personal loss steers us away from embracing the beauty of a conscious physical death. Birthing into spirit isn't normally a part of the journey for most personalities. We have not been taught that physical death is a part of the journey of the incarnated soul. Most personalities have imprinted that death takes our loved ones away from us, thus death is to be feared. Because of this fear we miss the gift of holding space for our loved one who is leaving the physical and birthing into spirit.

Most of us can recall reading or hearing about how someone has defied the norm and experienced what is often seen as a mystical experience. These people have had a near death experience and experienced heaven, or seen an angel, or experienced a physical miracle. Physical consciousness tells us that this is not the norm. In a world which sees and experiences life through the lens of physical consciousness we have somehow created a world which is void of spiritual experiences as part of the norm.

Physical consciousness as we know it in the era of 2014 is shifting. It's been shifting and since the energetic shift in December of 2012 spiritual consciousness is breaking through the old beliefs and paradigms. Personalities are moving into expanded states of consciousness. People want to talk about soul. People are asking, "What is the soul? How do I connect with my soul? Is there really life after death?"

For those who are ready to walk through the door into another consciousness, spirit consciousness, a whole new world awaits you. This expanded state of consciousness occurs for many of us every day, but we miss the signs. We miss the experiences of spiritual consciousness because we are focused on physical consciousness.

There are signs all around us supporting heaven, an afterlife, and supporting more to this life than we experience through physical consciousness. As we shift into spiritual consciousness we will begin to embrace that there is more to life than being born, living and dying, much more.

It is to the subject of birthing into spirit I now turn for the next part of this book. I believe that by viewing death through spiritual consciousness we can create a new paradigm shift which allows for the mystical to be the new norm. By embracing physical death as a part of the journey of the incarnated soul we can begin to embrace death as part of this journey not the end of the journey. Death doesn't have to be something which takes our loved ones away from us.

Personalities who are transitioning from physical consciousness to spiritual consciousness begin seeing with a new sight. They begin seeing through the eyes of someone who, given the opportunity, will share the experience with others. The stories I share with you in the next few chapters each share a gift and a message that was learned while living and birthing into spirit. Each person has a message, one I hope which will inspire you to perhaps expand your consciousness about the dying experience.

The first stories I want to share with you about death took place when I was a little girl around the age of eight to nine. I was very confused about death. The elders in my tribe didn't talk about death. I only knew it made people cry. It was confusing to see people crying at funerals. Couldn't they see the angels that were everywhere? Couldn't they see grandpa surrounded by others?

The elders tried to tell me the stiff cold body in the coffin was my grandpa Mummert. I knew it wasn't true. I could still see Pop and he wasn't stiff and cold. Pop was beautiful in his body of light. He tried his best to console his children and loved ones who mourned his death. "Why couldn't they see him?" I wondered.

When my grandpa Hoke died, it was even worse. Unlike grandpa Mummert who had been sick and died peacefully, no one told us why grandpa Hoke died. I remember the day like it was yesterday. My uncle George came for my mom. They were whispering and then I heard my mom crying. She went with him. I remember watching them leave as they drove down the driveway. I knew something bad had occurred.

We were told that grandpa died. When we went to his funeral the casket was standing inside the church to the left hand side. It was shut. This time no one was going to force me to touch the cold hard body, but I wondered why we couldn't see him. The angels were again everywhere. They were trying their best to console people. I tried to tell my sister Debbie about the angels, but she shushed me. I remember sitting in the church watching the angels. I don't remember seeing my grandpa on that day. I do remember others were there who I now understand had crossed over. They were doing their best to try to comfort everyone. This was all confusing, people crying. I wondered why they were crying. Death wasn't bad. I could see the angels and departed loved ones. I now understand everyone around me had been focused on physical consciousness.

I found out a few days later from cruel friends how my grandpa had died. I didn't understand. I do know his death was the turning point in my life when I began to believe what I was told about death. I also know that this was the time in my life when I began to view the world and my life through physical consciousness. Seeing angels and departed loved ones would now occur only on rare occasions, and would not fully resurface for thirty years. It was only after a soul realignment (I call it a soul boot.) that I began to bring forth spiritual consciousness, thus began seeing angels again.

Slowly over time I began to understand that death wasn't something to fear and death wasn't bad. I wanted to change the way personalities viewed death and the dying process. The physical deaths of my dad, my beloved soul companion Johnny and my sister gave me opportunity to put to test my own personal beliefs which had evolved considerably since I was that little girl standing in the church wondering why no one could see that death wasn't bad.

Believing that there is only physical death and that we are incarnated souls has shaped my beliefs about death. I believe that the birthing into spirit journey is one which can heal and transform everyone whose life is being touched by the physical death of a loved one. I do not mean to imply that when someone we love births into spirit we will not experience sadness and grief. Death brings great change into our lives. Even when we know that our loved one still experiences consciousness in this place many call heaven we miss having them in our lives.

I now share the stories of several people who have birthed into spirit. I'm going to ask each of you who read our words to be willing and open to a consciousness shift as you read this book. Each of the stories shared are true. Each personality experienced birthing into spirit the way they had lived their life. Birthing into spirit offers gifts for everyone, from the person who is dying a physical death to everyone who enters the room of the person birthing into spirit. Their stories are meant to inspire you as well as give you insight into the birthing into spirit experience. The lessons they learned even as they birthed into spirit are lessons we each have the opportunity to learn as we live our lives.

CHAPTER THREE

I CAME BACK FOR ME

I want to share with you a story of a beautiful man I met at the York House Hospice for AIDS. By this time angels were once again a major part of my life and I had begun to shift into seeing my world through the eyes of spirit consciousness. At the time I didn't understand that through the soul realignment I had experienced years earlier I had shifted my sight and my heart to embrace the world of spirit.

The hospice was a safe haven for those dying of AIDS. There was much ignorance about AIDS in 2002. The hospice staff treated everyone with dignity and love. Those who cared for the patients gave excellent comfort care. However, none of the nurses were trained in how to care for the incarnating soul as it began the process of letting go of the physical. In

2014 this is still the case. The need for birthing into spirit coaches continues to grow.

Time and time again I would hear someone trying to tell a nurse, a loved one or friend who came to visit, about seeing people in their room who had transitioned, died. Those birthing into spirit would speak about the angels they were seeing in their rooms. I would hear the well-meaning nurse, family member or friend tell the person that they didn't see anything or anyone in the room. It was often a point of frustration for those who were birthing into spirit. They tried to tell others what they were seeing but to no avail. A birthing into spirit coach would honor the experiences.

I remember talking to the director of the hospice asking her to talk to the staff about denying those transitioning their experience. I explained every chance I got to anyone who would listen that their loved one was "seeing" with a different sight. I understand today that they were experiencing spiritual consciousness. The filter which once masked their sight was now taken away as those who were birthing into spirit began to experience more and more of spiritual consciousness as they prepared to leave the physical life.

Having the gift of clear sight I could see what many of the nurses and family members could not see. The rooms of the hospice were indeed filled with light beings and those who had crossed over.

Sam (not his real name) was someone I had grown attached to. We shared a special connection from the moment we met. I now understand that Sam and I had a soul contract to teach each other. Our soul contract was clear, "I will be that which you need me to be so you can be that which you need to be." Sam and I had grown close as I held space for him to talk about his life. I quickly discovered that Sam was a gay man who never came out to his family. Sam wouldn't allow himself to talk freely about death with his family because he had never talked freely about life with them. He was dying the way he lived, holding everything in, pleasing others and fearing that he would be punished for being gay.

They never talked about how he contracted AIDS. In fact, like most families, they never talked about anything that would upset his parents. His mother spent time by her son's bedside. She loved her son, this was clear. It was also clear that she did not know her son. Somehow Sam had grown up to believe that his mother's love was conditional, so he wore a mask, covering his authentic self from those in his tribe. Sam continued to do what he did during his life, try to protect his mother. It was clear they loved each other, but really didn›t know each other beyond the mask each used for protection.

Sam had incarnated into a family who said they loved him but didn't see him. He was raised putting on different masks, performing for those around him. He did so because of learned behavior and living an unconscious life. Sam had learned as all children do how to please the members of his family. He adopted his family's emotional resonance and never grew into his own. At the age of thirty he was still pleasing everyone around him. He even tried to cling to life because his mother begged him to fight. It seemed very important to Sam that he continue pleasing his family even as he birthed into spirit. He wouldn't or couldn't allow himself to be honest with his family even as his body shut down.

I remember one particular night at the hospice. Sam's body was growing weaker and we were sitting out on the porch. Sam had his head on my shoulder. He was exhausted, physically, spiritually and emotionally. He knew I could see angels and he always wanted to know if one was watching over him. On this night I could see the angel of death was hovering around us.

I knew if Sam was ready to let go of the physical he could go with this beautiful angel. I understood that this beautiful angel was going to show Sam the way back home, into the light.

Unknown to me at the time the patient in the room who could see out her window to the back porch was telling her nurse, "Do you see them, angels everywhere." The patient kept pointing to the back porch but the nurse kept telling her there were only Sam and me on the porch. A birthing into spirit coach would have honored what the patient was saying. I told Sam I could see the angel and if he was ready he could let go, leave the physical and go into the light. We had had many talks about "heaven" before this night. Sam was sure he would go to "hell" because he was gay. He even believed as many people did that AIDS was his punishment. Sam once asked me if I believed in heaven. I told him I did. I also told him that I didn't believe in hell as a place you go to after death. I believed and still believe hell is an experience one has because they see themselves separated from Creator God.

I told Sam on that night the angel of death was there to help him go back into the light. Sam's body was so weak. He knew his mother wasn't ready for him to die and had been pleading with him to fight for his life. It was clear Sam had no fight left in him. The light and love from the angel was all consuming.

I could feel Sam's breath beginning to relax and suddenly I could feel his life force leave his physical body. I'm not sure how long we sat there, but I knew by his lifeless body that Sam had birthed into spirit. Peacefully, and calmly Sam let go of his physical body. There was peace, nothing but peace sitting there holding Sam in my arms. I don't know how long we sat there but suddenly I realized Sam's mother had come to the porch and she could see her son had died. She came over to his lifeless body and began crying and pleading. She said, "No Sam, no," over and over as she shook his arm. Suddenly with a huge force of energy we heard Sam's lifeless body fighting for air and with one huge wave of energy he was breathing again. I couldn't believe what had just occurred. Sam had come back to life because his mother wouldn't let him go, or at least that's what I thought at the time.

We gently took Sam back to his bed and over the next two weeks Sam and his mother did what they had not been able to do during his life, they talked. Sam never got out of bed after the event on the porch but something in Sam had changed.

He told me later that after his spirit left his body he felt free, something he had never experienced in life. Sam told me that he had gone with the beautiful angel and had moved through a beautiful tunnel. He said that he went to heaven and was there until he felt a pull of energy pulling him back through the tunnel of light back into his physical body. Sam said he was surprised to have found out later that he was only gone minutes, because while on the other side he had had time for a life review. Sam said he believed he came back, not for his mother but for himself. Sam experienced a near death experienced that night. He was given a brief do over, meaning after having a life review with his counsel of wisdom Sam came back and began to live authentically. During his life review Sam saw how he had not seized the opportunities during his life to embrace freedom. During his life review he was shown that freedom was one of the life lessons his soul had planned for his life.

Sam realized he had never known freedom. He had made many of his life choices in fear. He was given the choice to stay in heaven or return to the physical and have what few of us get, a chance at a brief do over.

He came back for only two weeks. During his last two weeks of life Sam lived authentically. He did from his birthing into spirit bed what he could not do during his life. HE WAS AUTHENTIC. Sam talked openly and freely about his life, who he was and yes the regrets he had about not living authentically during his life.

Sam didn't allow others to see him until after a Near Death Experience (NDE). Sam did not waste one moment of time after his NDE. His used his NDE to heal many wounded parts that he had kept buried during his life.

Whatever happened to Sam that night I know he was different. He stopped taking care of his mother and those around him. He admitted being gay. His family of course, already knowing this continued to love him. Sam was no longer afraid of death and he had a peace around him that was surreal.

Sam died peacefully about two weeks after the event on the porch without his mother by his bedside. She had finally left the room to get some needed sleep and he died. Sam peacefully left his physical body and birthed into spirit.

I received a call from one of the nurses who asked me if I wanted to see Sam one last time. I did, and when I got there Rick another hospice patient wanted to see his friend one last time. Together we sat by Sam's bed and recalled the experiences we had all shared with our beloved friend. Rick said, "Miss Kate it feels so peaceful." Rick shared with us that Sam had told him not to be afraid of dying. Sam had shared with Rick how beautiful it was in heaven. After Rick left the room the nurse and I washed Sam's body. Of course we did this for ourselves. The nurse was the same nurse who had been with the patient two weeks earlier who said she saw the angels. She was focused on physical consciousness. She was an excellent caregiver. She was not a good birthing into spirit coach. While we were washing Sam's body the nurse began to cry. She said, "Sam is standing next to you." She was in awe because even though Sam's body laid there lifeless she could feel and see his essence. I could too and I thanked Sam for making his presence known to us that day.

Seeing Sam's soul essence so shortly after death is not unusual. After physical death the departed loved one will often hover around the body which had been the home for the journey of the soul. Being free of the physical does not stop those who have birthed into spirit caring about those they have left behind. Sam had birthed into spirit and he was free. Sam taught me a lot during our time together. The biggest gift he gave me is helping me to understand it's never too late to be authentic with those in my tribe or anyone else.

Sam also gives the gift of freedom to us.

It took a NDE and a life review to help Sam understand that part of his soul's life plan was to experience freedom in this life. Sam missed many opportunities to embrace freedom during his life. After his NDE Sam understood that it's never too late to embrace freedom.

Not everyone is fortunate to have a NDE and a life review before they birth into spirit. Ask yourself what areas of your life do you want to change TODAY so you can begin to experience FREEDOM. Ask yourself in what areas of your life and with who are you not being authentic.

Here's a suggestion. Begin to create a world which is safe to bring forth the "REAL" you. Choose a life that is authentic. Throw away the mask and the people who you have in your life who you cannot be authentic with.

Today choose FREEDOM. Sam did.

After Sam transitioned there were more deaths, more loss, but also experiences where those involved had opportunities to grow, or not.

The environment at the hospice was a loving one. The director was a woman of vision and prided herself in pain management and created an environment which offered support for all those involved. For me, my experience at the hospice was a turning point in my life. I loved helping people transition from this life to the afterlife. I was good at it, however, what I learned from my experiences at the hospice was people died the way they lived. If someone lived a life of fear they usually were afraid of death. I decided to dedicate my life to helping people live a conscious life, meaning live a life without fear and teaching others about the world of spirit.

My journey took me away from hospice and eventually I began doing energy work and teaching classes about soul and about there being more, much more to the human experience.

CHAPTER FOUR

THE ETERNAL PRESENT MOMENT

I met Lana through my spiritual director. Lana was a devoted Christian and I wasn't sure if we would connect. Our mutual love of Jesus and her sincere desire to heal took us on a journey which would change both of our lives. Lana was not given a good prognosis by her doctors so she started looking into alternative therapies. I was an energy practitioner at the time. Lana and I both had the same spiritual director. He was also a Christian as well as a Lutheran minister.

I began giving Lana energy sessions and we would talk about Jesus. As time went on she healed and despite the doctor's grim prognosis she regained her health. When someone receives a healing, as Lana did, I always tell them, now go and change your life. I believe that illness, in adults, is always an opportunity for soul growth. Most doctors and spiritual leaders have little understanding of the ways of the soul. They do not view disease as an opportunity for soul growth.

My understanding of soul is different. I believe that we are all incarnated souls and we are spiritual beings who choose to experience growth on the earth planes of consciousness. I see the physical body as the vehicle our souls choose for this journey on earth. Our bodies know only perfect health. I view disease as a message from our soul that the personality has made choices which were not in alignment with the soul's life plan. Disease is also an indication of soul essence loss.

As in the case of Lana her cancer began in her uterus telling me that she had blocked the creative energy of her soul as well as her emotions. Through our sessions and time together Lana understood how she had become boxed in with her thinking and her life and would seek to change this.

Time went by and we stayed in touch. About two years after meeting Lana she called me and asked if she could bring a gingerbread house for my grandchildren to enjoy. I will never forget that day. I offered her a session and as I moved my hands around her body I began to feel cancer. I was concerned. I knew Lana was leaving the next day for a trip to Florida so I said nothing. I must also admit, I was hoping I was wrong. Unfortunately I was not wrong. Lana called me from Florida and said she had to go to the hospital because she was feeling exhausted. The doctors discovered the cancer had returned.

Lana began many different forms of alternative therapies. She even went to New York and began using food as medicine, but to no benefit. In July, six months after that day I felt the return of the cancer Lana asked me to begin energy sessions. She said the doctors held no hope for her physical healing. We agreed on that day that we would both focus on her physical healing until she told me otherwise.

About two weeks later as I was giving Lana an energy session she said, "Katye it's that time. Tomorrow I'm going to call hospice and I need you to help me die."

I must admit I wasn't ready to give up. However I honored Lana's wishes and we began to shift into what I call birthing into spirit. She gathered her support team and I was one of them. I was her birthing into spirit coach. Lana spoke to family members and decided who she wanted to support her during this grand adventure into birthing into spirit. Her daughter and brother were supportive of her decisions. Her sisters were convinced that having me as her guide was not in alignment with their Christian beliefs. After several stressful visits and calls Lana cut off communication with those she felt were not supportive of her choices.

Lana had been a teacher for most of her life. She continued teaching even as she began focusing on leaving the earth planes of consciousness. I helped to set the environment in which Lana could focus her energy on leaving the physical world and her body.

With her hospice team in place and her physical needs taken care of Lana could begin focusing on birthing into spirit. As her birthing into spirit coach I helped create space which helped Lana begin the process of letting go of the physical. She received daily energy sessions which helped to relax her body as well as her mind. She also read her Bible every day. She listened to music she loved and enjoyed looking outside. From her bed she could see the deer and her beautiful gardens. Through guided meditations I taught her how to travel to different planes of consciousness. It didn't take Lana long to begin traveling to the other side on her own. She simply had to be taught that it was possible to do so. She talked freely about what and who she saw in "heaven".

I went every day to give her an energy session. Our focus now turned to talking about Lana birthing back into spirit. Lana had a conscious dying process. She talked about her love of God and Jesus. She would tell us about how she traveled through this beautiful tunnel during sleep time and on the other side she was seeing departed loved ones. I remember one day she was confused and she told her daughter she kept seeing Mike on the other side. This confused Lana. She knew that Mike had been sick but she had not known that he had died two weeks earlier. Lana kept saying how great Mike looked. As Lana moved more into spiritual sight she began seeing angels in her room while awake. She was amazed that she could now see angels and departed loved ones while awake and while asleep. Lana continued going back and forth between the earth planes of consciousness and the astral planes. She simply described the astral planes as heaven. She would talk about seeing Jesus in heaven and how beautiful it was where she was going. She said Jesus was different in heaven. She loved his laughter.

Lana had asked me to give her eulogy at her celebration of life service. She was clear she wanted a celebration of her life. She chose the songs, scriptures and those she wanted to speak. With me her instructions were clear. She wanted people to learn that all we had was the eternal present moment. She said that nothing mattered but the eternal present moment. Lana said, "Don't look back, it's wasted time." She also said looking forward may never come. The eternal present moment and staying present in that moment was her core teaching.

Lana continued talking about heaven but her message of teaching people to stay in the eternal present moment took on new energy as she traveled freely between planes of consciousness. Everyday Lana would talk about the importance of people getting it, staying in the eternal present moment. She would try and explain that in the eternal present moment there was no past, no future only the NOW. Lana said by focusing on the NOW one could enter a state of grace. At the time I don't think I fully got what Lana was teaching but today I get it. The eternal has no beginning and it has no end.

I knew I was not going to be with Lana when she birthed into spirit. The last time I saw her I kissed her forehead and she smiled. She said, "I'm going home to Jesus. I understand now what my faith could not teach me." She was connected to something few experience during life. Lana had a peace which surpassed all human understanding for in death she found life, ever-lasting life. There was no fear as she moved freely back and forth between worlds, only love, only peace. She knew that even after physical death she would still experience consciousness in heaven.

I wasn't surprised when I received the phone call from her daughter that her mother had transitioned. Her daughter said they had just given her a massage, one Lana had requested. Lana loved the touch of her daughter's hands and made remarks how good it felt to be touched. She was awake and alert during the massage. After the massage she asked her brother and daughter if they could see the angels. They could not but they felt the peace in the room. They both left the room to get something to eat and heard a sound over the baby-com. When they entered the room they knew that Lana had birth into spirit. They both said even though her body was lifeless they could still feel her presence in the room.

Lana was another one of my teachers. Our soul contracts had brought us together. I feel her presence as I type these words and she reminds me once again to tell people to focus on the eternal present moment.

She reminds us that in the eternal moment there is no history, no past, no present, just the now. Lana's message and gift to us was clear. Focus on the eternal present moment and in that moment you will find peace which surpasses all understanding.

By focusing on the present one puts their energy on BEING fully present, bringing all your focus, attention and energy to the ETERNAL PRESENT MOMENT. Lana was convinced that people who were not birthing into spirit could learn what it took her until she began shifting her consciousness from physical consciousness to spiritual consciousness to learn.

Lana discovered by focusing on the NOW, the ETERNAL PRESENT MOMENT, the past didn't matter. She gave no energy to the past; it did not exist in the ETERNAL PRESENT MOMENT. All the pain, the wounds, the memories meant nothing in the NOW.

Lana's message is clear; by focusing on the ETERNAL PRESENT MOMENT we can each enter into this place she had found during her birthing into spirit. In this PLACE of the NOW there was nothing but love, grace and peace. Lana didn't care anymore about the past and all the plans she had made and never stepped into for many reasons, the past had no energy, nor did the regrets she once had about choices made. She was in the NOW, the ETERNAL PRESENT MOMENT and this is the way she lived her life as she birthed fully into spirit.

Everyone who visited her during this time left her room feeling, cleansed, renewed and at peace. What we didn't know at the time was Lana had created space for each one of us to enter the NOW with her. Her faith and her understanding of the ETERNAL PRESENT MOMENT were so strong that those who visited her entered what I can only describe as a state of grace.

Lana's message was clear. If we focused on the ETERNAL PRESENT MOMENT we can live our lives in a state of grace that surpasses all human understanding.

Today I invite you to fully bring your consciousness to the ETERNAL PRESENT MOMENT, the NOW. Take a few deep breaths and allow your consciousness and your energy to enter that place where nothing exists but LOVE. In this place of love there is no past, no future only the NOW. Allow the energy of the NOW, the ETERNAL PRESENT MOMENT to enter every cell, tissue and organ of your body. With each breath you take allow the energy of the ETERNAL PRESENT MOMENT to enter all that you are.

In this place you will experience what Lana experienced while she birthed into spirit. The gift, the teachings of Lana are clear. There is truly nothing but the ETERNAL PRESENT MOMENT.

CHAPTER FIVE

I MET THE REAL JESUS

My father, David Nelson Mummert, taught me many lessons. Our journey as father and daughter took us in many twists and turns of life. When I was a little girl my dad would say many times that I was different than his other children. When I was a little girl different was not a good thing. Six years before my father birthed into spirit he was once again saying that I was different from his other children. This time he meant it in a positive way.

My dad's own journey had been one which at times was difficult however no matter what life threw at him my dad had his faith. He loved Jesus with his whole heart. We were raised going to church every Sunday but my dad also lived his faith. He was known to go out of his way to help those in need. He was a good man, a man of faith and through the years his faith would be challenged but he never wavered.

For dad, Jesus was the way the truth and the light. As his children grew and adopted their own beliefs dad was challenged to the core. I remember one time my mom called me to come up and talk to daddy. He was sitting alone in the basement and was crying. He had found out the night before that two of my brothers had very different religious beliefs from his. This shook daddy to the core.

My dad was overwhelmed with grief. He said, "Katye what did I do wrong, my boys will go to hell if they don't accept Jesus as their savior." I remember telling daddy that my brothers were good men and I believed that if Jesus judged them at all it would be by their works and lives instead of their following a religion.

As life went on my dad seemed to accept his children including me and honored our chosen paths. I'm sure he prayed everyday of his life for all of us to accept Jesus into our lives and hearts. The years passed. I was blessed to get to know the man my dad had become as he aged. He had supported my choices by loving me even when he didn't understand them. One day my mom heard him talking to his fishing buddies about me. Dad told his buddies that his daughter Katye talked to angels, and then he was heard saying but what's really special is they talk to her.

Living next door to my parents they could see I had stopped going to church. My parents both knew I was teaching and offering spiritual healing. My dad never asked me what I was doing but one day when he asked me to give him an energy session I did. From that day forward my dad became an energy junkie. He said he didn't know what I did but he felt loved and at peace when my hands were on him. One day he even said, when I die I want your hands on me. Little did I know how his request would affect my life years later.

In 2004 Dad was diagnosed with colon cancer. I had felt the presence of the cancer during a session and it felt angry. The doctors had not offered daddy much hope past living six months but he lived five more years. During those five years dad received many energy sessions and our bond grew even stronger.

I will never forget the Christmas gathering with my brothers and sisters as daddy told everyone of his decision to stop all treatment and call in hospice. There our family sat trying hard to support our dad's decision, each one asking questions. I'm sure each one of us was having our own inner dialogue. Mom sat next to daddy, tissue in her hand, a tear slowly flowing down her face. Here was her husband of sixty years saying he was ready to die. Dad said he had lived a good life and he was tired, tired of the treatments, and tired of the pain.

We agreed as a family we would support him and his decision to call in hospice. Two months later dad had me make the call to his doctor requesting hospice.

Dad's doctor had been his family doctor since a young man right out of med school. They had known each other for over forty years. They had a mutual respect for one another. His doctor did not agree with dad's decision to call in hospice. He called dad and tried to talk him out of it. When that didn't work he even made a home visit. He assured dad that he could live longer, maybe even a year. He encouraged daddy to keep fighting. Dad had no fight left in him. He was ready to die. Dad had told me that it would be torture being an old man sitting in a rocking chair unable to do the things he loved. I called the cancer doctor the next day and asked if they would arrange for hospice care. They didn't want to go over his physical doctor but said they would talk to him. They did and a few days later the hospice angels came out to do an interview and to set things in motion. Later that afternoon they came with all the equipment including a hospital bed. That night would be the last night he would sleep with his beloved Kathryn.

Early the next morning daddy made his way to the bed that would become his birthing into spirit bed. I can only imagine how daddy felt as he walked into the living room toward the hospice bed. It seemed with each step he became weaker and weaker. My mom and my brother George each supported a side. Mom's face was white and I can only imagine what she was feeling as they made their way to the bed which dad would call home until the day he died.

The hospice team of nurses assured us that dad was nowhere near death. In fact my brother Jim said they told him by their assessment dad had many months of life left in him. Our brother Gene was on vacation and Jim assured him he could stay; there was no need to rush home. Little did the nurses or my brothers know of dad's resolve to die. He was clear. He was ready to die.

Thinking back to this time I can clearly see how this time was a defining moment for our family. I had seen through the years that dying brought out the best and the worst of families. Time would tell what this journey with dad would bring out in our family.

We quickly agreed as a family that we wouldn't let mom alone with daddy. There we sat, supporting dad as best we could. Daddy and I had had many talks about life and death especially during the past five years as he lived with cancer. Dad's faith was strong, but daddy had never been known for his patience. Little did we know daddy's patience with death would be challenged during the next few weeks.

My brother George lived in Missouri and had to go home soon. Dad told him not to worry he would be dead in a couple of days. Thinking back on this statement I find myself laughing because daddy thought that he could will himself to die.

After a few days daddy decided he couldn't die because my brother Gene was on vacation. I kid you not, daddy believed he needed all of his children surrounding him and then he could die. The nurses again told my brother Jim who relayed the information to my brother Gene that daddy's vitals were strong and that he was nowhere near death. Daddy was so sure the only thing keeping him alive was that Gene wasn't home.

During this time my dad began working on what I called birthing into spirit. I had explained to daddy that he was going back and forth between planes of consciousness during his sleep time. Dad's visual memories of the other side began to be very detailed. Dad was doing from his bed what he could no longer do in waking state. Dad was building his home in heaven.

Daddy was clear about his home in what he called heaven. Every day he talked about his home on the other side. As the days went on daddy began seeing departed loved ones and even saw his beloved dogs which had died.

One day daddy said, "If you could see where I'm going you would all want to go with me." He even told mom, "Honey it's beautiful where I'm going." Dad told mom, "I wish you could go with me but they told me our children need you to stay with them for a while longer." He told mom not to worry that she would join him someday and they would be together in heaven.

As the days went on daddy began to drift into dreamtime. He always seemed peaceful as he slept. When he woke up his details of heaven were clear. He woke up, one day and was saying, "Mommy, oh mommy." My mom rushed to his side and said "Honey I'm here," thinking he was crying out for her. Daddy said, "No I was calling out to my mommy, she was there, I was with her." A tear fell from his eyes as he described how beautiful his mom looked. Dad was very emotional as he described his visit on the other side with his mom. He said, he hadn't wanted to leave her but his mom said, it wasn't his time yet. She told him, "Soon, very soon we will be together."

Dad's mom had died when he was seven. Daddy had once told me that when you grow up without a mom you miss something. He said, he had aunts who loved him as a boy and sisters who tried to mother him but without having a mom he had grown up feeling he was missing something. He was clear that when he died he would once again be with his mom.

After seeing his mom, it seemed like daddy had a new resolve to birth into spirit. He talked to my brother Gene on the phone and told him if he would come home he knew he could die. Dad was clear; he could not die without being with all his children. My brother George needed to go back to Missouri and my brother Gary was coming from Washington. Again my brother Jim assured Gene, dad was not near death. I told Jim, I believed daddy only had a few weeks to live. The nurses did not agree, nor did his family doctor. Gene ended his trip and came home.

Daddy was happy. He told my brother George once Gene got home he could die. Based on this George extended his stay.

As a family when supported dad's being able to talk about his dreams. He kept telling us they weren't dreams that he was visiting heaven when he was sleeping. To prove his point one day daddy said, "Well I'm not going to die today." He said, "Too many people are in line in front of me." When the newspaper came he asked to see it. He went straight to the obituaries and said, "See I told you, look at all the people who died."

Dad was happy that Gene came home. He believed once he saw Gene he would die. When Gene arrived we gathered by his bedside. Dad had talked to each one of us and said, "OK, now I can die." He closed his eyes and in silence we sat there, waiting. After about ten minutes daddy said, "I don't know what's wrong, I can't die." He said, "You might as well get some rest it's not going to happen today."

The next day he called his family doctor; he was clear now that his family doctor wasn't letting him go. When the doctor got on the phone daddy thanked him for being a good doctor. He told him it was time to let him go. After this call daddy was sure he would now die. It had been about two weeks since the morning he had made his way into his birthing into spirit bed.

I had told daddy that birthing into spirit was as hard as being born. That in some ways it was harder because leaving so many loved ones and the physical life was hard. I told him to keep looking for the light and allow the light to be his guide.

One day daddy wanted to talk about Jesus. It seems dad had seen Jesus on the other side. His words were clear. Having loved and followed Jesus his whole life he was amazed that he had met the real Jesus. Dad told us, "I met the real Jesus last night. Not the Jesus they taught me about in church but the real Jesus." Daddy said, "I now understand that my children who didn't follow Jesus had known the truth about Jesus all along."

He said, "Gary and George have been better Christians than I have been because they understood about the real Jesus." Daddy was clear and in awe of having met the real Jesus.

During the time we spent waiting for daddy to birth into spirit there were many moments of joy. Dad would have it no other way. One evening when several of his grandchildren and great grandchildren were there daddy said, "Lets have an ice cream party." He said, "I'm dying, I'm going home so lets celebrate!" Trust me, none of us felt like celebrating. Dad said he wanted butter pecan ice cream. My mom told him, "Honey you haven't been eating." Daddy said, "Katye said the dying can have whatever they want. I want ice cream." I still laugh as I remember my daughter Kathy going to get him ice cream. They smashed the pecans up and stirred the ice cream until it was soft. With spoon in his hand daddy said, "Everyone, I love you." Seeing the sad looks on his grandchildren's faces daddy said, "Come on it's a celebration, I'm dying." After he ate the soft ice cream he looked at my daughter and said, "Give me another dish of ice cream, this time make it the real stuff." Again, we couldn›t help but laugh; daddy was happy, surrounded by his loved ones.

That evening around 1:00AM I received a phone call from my brother George. He said, "Daddy was dying. Come now." My brother Gary was home from Washington so dad was sure this was it. All he needed was all of his children to be by his bedside. By 2:00AM we had all gathered by his bedside except my sister Sara. There we were, mom, Jim, Gene, Debbie, Gary, George and myself. Daddy said, "I love all of you and I would like to have another year or so, but who wouldn't." Suddenly he asked where Sara was. Sara was the baby of the family and she was dad's little girl. I called her and she said, I didn't think he was really dying, if you think he is I'll come. I told daddy this and he said, "Ah hell you might as well go home. She's right I'm not going to die tonight." This time he blamed it on Sara.

Before going home I talked to daddy and he said he couldn't figure out why he couldn't die. I told him, daddy your body has to shut down. He said, "You never told me that." I still smile as he realized at that moment that he could not will himself to die.

As I walked home I remember reaching out to an old pastor who daddy had loved and admired. Pastor Will had died a few years earlier and I simply asked him to help daddy.

The next morning dad was very excited to tell us about seeing Pastor Will on the other side. Dad said, Pastor Will told him, "David, you must be patient. You never have learned patience and the good lord wants you to learn it now." Dad understood what Pastor Will had told him about learning patience. After his visit from heaven with Pastor Will dad seemed more content.

George and Gary returned home the next day with reassurances that dad was stable. Little did any of us know that dad now had a plan. One morning a few days after dad saw Pastor Will I went over to relieve my brother Jim. I kissed daddy on the check and said, "I love you, pop." He said, "I love you, girly." I didn't know at the time those would be the last words my dad would speak. Around 7:30 my mom woke up and came to dad's bedside. She kissed him and said, "I love you honey." I still remember the look on her face as she realized he was not going to respond. She looked at me with the look of apprehension not knowing what to do. A tear flowed from her eye and she held his hand tight. Finally when she was sure he wouldn't respond she left his bedside.

This was the beginning of daddy allowing his body to shut down. Gone were the days of laughter, and messages about heaven. No more twinkles were to be seen in his eyes for he never opened them again. We continued to hold space for daddy was now birthing into spirit. We continued taking turns sitting by his bed as his breathing became more labored and shallow at times. We continued to talk to daddy, believing at some level of his consciousness he could hear us. I kept telling him to go into the light.

I had decided and kept telling everyone I wouldn't be with daddy when he crossed over. Truth is I wasn't ready for daddy to die. I did my best to hold space for dad and mom but the heart of my little girl was breaking. I wanted more time with my dad and I didn't want to be there when he died.

A few days went by and now it was clear dad's body was shutting down. His breathing had taken on a rhythm of its own. Sometimes it seemed moments between breaths. The dance to free his soul essence from his physical body was hard at times to watch. As a family we continued to hold space for daddy. I'm sure each one of us who sat by his bedside was filled with thoughts of this man we knew and loved. Each one of us did what we could to support daddy birthing into spirit.

My brother Gary had taken the night shift. My brother Jim who had only missed three nights since daddy began his journey of birthing into spirit had gone home, for some much needed rest. I was sleeping on the sofa. Around 3:00AM I switched places with my brother Gary who was sitting by daddy's chair. Around 5:00AM Gary said he was going home. I told him, daddy is going to die before sunrise. He kissed daddy one last time, clearly he did not want to be there when daddy died. I began singing dad's favorite songs. During this time I saw my mom come out and lie on the sofa. She laid with her face turned toward the back of the sofa and covered her head. I continued singing and through tears sang "I walk in the Garden with Jesus" and then I sang, "It is well with my Soul".

I looked at daddy, this man I loved who taught me well during our time together. I knew what I had to do. I put my hand close to his shoulder and said, "Daddy I can bear witness to your final breath, go into the light, go home with Jesus." My father took one last breath and I watched his spirit leave his body. My daddy's beautiful spirit was released from his body and now, his spirit would make the journey into the light, from which he came many years ago.

Before telling my mom that daddy had birthed into spirit I called my husband. I didn't know at the time but he had already been awakened by his first wife who had died eighteen years earlier. Jane told Allan I needed him that my dad had died.

Dad knew his death would be hard on mom. He called mom his angel. As I looked over to the sofa I could now see that my dad's soul essence was in the room, hovering around my mother. It was surreal, my dad's body laid there lifeless but I could still see his light essence. As many souls do daddy wanted to watch over mom during this time. I slowly walked over to the sofa and before I could say anything mom said, "I know he died." She asked me why I hadn't wakened her and I told her it was clear she hadn't wanted to witness his last breath. She agreed.

As my brothers and sisters arrived at the house it was now my time to become a daughter and to allow others to take over. Until the time of dad's transition I had tried my best to be caregiver and his birthing into spirit coach. I had done what I knew my dad needed me to do to help him birth into spirit. For some reason I was to be with my dad and bear witness to his last breath. Now I would allow myself to feel his loss, in the physical.

Six years have passed since my dad birthed into spirit. During this time I have continued to have contact with my dad. Even before the death of my dad I believed in an afterlife. The way dad shared with us during the last three weeks of his life was a gift to everyone who talked to him. His descriptions of heaven and those he saw in heaven were said by a man who believed he was going home. My dad was a devoted Christian all of his life. He believed that with the second coming of Jesus he would rise again. His experiences convinced him that he had met the real Jesus. The one they didn't teach about in church. He had found peace and he was ready to leave those of us he loved.

My dad had experienced what I call conscious dying. This was only possible because we made space for dad to share his experiences as he was birthing back into spirit. When daddy entered the hospital bed three weeks before he died he did so with the intent to birth into spirit. His doctor and the caring hospice workers felt he had months to live. Dad had a different plan.

Dad had talked through the years about a pastor he knew and respected who had decided he too would die on his own terms. Like my dad, this pastor chose the day and time he would begin to refuse food and water. Daddy was clear; he was ready to leave the physical body which no longer served him. Both men knew they had to take dying into their own hands. They knew the current laws did not allow health care that would assist their bodies to shut down with grace. They had to do it themselves. I continue to think about the courage and energy it takes for someone to close their eyes and refuse food and water much less to stop talking to loved ones. My dad, like his pastor starved himself to death and we as a family watched helpless everyday as daddy's body slowly shut down.

Again I witnessed that one dies the way they lived. Of course there was sadness about leaving his wife, family and friends but daddy was ready to leave the physical. He knew without doubt loved ones who had birthed into spirit were waiting for him to join them in the world of spirit. My dad had lived a rich life and had experienced soul growth and soul expansion, of this I am sure. I think the words so elegantly written many years ago sum up the journey of my dad.

"When peace, like a river, attendeth my way, When sorrows like sea billows roll; Whatever my lot, Thou has taught me to say, it is well, it is well, with my soul. Refrain: it is well, with my soul, it is well, with my soul, it is well, it is well, with my soul."

Dad had no concept of being an incarnated soul. Somehow daddy understood that no matter what happens on this journey we call life, it is well, it is well with our souls.

The current laws in most states in the United States continue to deny people like my dad help with shutting the physical body down. His own doctor could not accept the fact that dad was ready to let go of the physical body which no longer allowed him to live a life of joy. The doctors would have continued treatment including radiation knowing that it would do nothing to cure the cancer. There needs to be a consciousness shift in regards to death with dignity. Laws denying medical assistance in regards to dying with dignity need to be changed. Doctors need to be educated about how to shift medical care into supportive care of the person birthing into spirit.

My dad had a great life. He loved his family and he loved life. He understood what his doctors did not; that letting go of physical life after all medical interventions have failed should be a choice, his choice.

The gifts and teachings of my dad were many both as he lived his life and as he birthed into spirit. I believe the greatest gift dad taught was FAITH. He had faith that his family would honor his choices concerning his ending his life on his terms. He also had FAITH that there was going to be life for him in a place he called heaven.

CHAPTER SIX

HEAVEN ISN'T A PLACE, HEAVEN IS GOD

I sit here and I ponder how to begin this chapter on Johnny. Since writing the book "Conscious Construction of the Soul," I understand Johnny and I had a sacred and binding soul contract. The many twists and turns of our lives brought us to the same location where we would meet. There was instant soul recognition, and our lives took on new meaning. I met Johnny at a nursing home in 1982.

When I met John I didn't have a concept of being an incarnated soul. I didn't know anything about soul contracts. Nor did I know that, although Johnny appeared to be limited, he was by far the most amazing, loving, angelic being I have ever met. I did know when I met Johnny my heart was connected to his. Little did I know that we would spend the next thirty years of our lives together. I quickly understood the only limitations Johnny had were those imposed on him from a world that could not see past his physical appearance.

The life lessons John taught those of us who were blessed to call him family were endless. During our thirty years of life together he was my teacher, my guide, my lover, my friend and my companion. The life lessons were many. Although he was limited by speech when he spoke, there was usually a profound message. John could say more with a look than most people could say with their words. I once asked him if he ever questioned why him? He answered, "Why not me."

During our life together, our bond would take us to the day where it was time for Johnny to begin his journey home, back into the light. Sitting here with tears flowing I must admit, since his birthing back into spirit my heart has never been the same. Someone once said that Johnny was the heart of our family. This was true and even though he is gone from our lives in the physical his essence still lives with each one of us.

Through the years Johnny's health slowly deteriorated. In October of 2011 Johnny had a mild heart attack. After this his energy level kept declining but his joy of life and spirit was strong. Johnny made the decision after his heart episode there would be no more hospitals, no more intrusive tests and no more interventions.

On January 17th 2012 John entered hospice care. His hospice experience on the whole was a good one.

Slowly over the months John began the journey back into spirit. He would talk about going back and forth between the world of physical and the world of spirit. He talked about my dad, David Nelson Mummert and said he was going to live with Pop on the other side. He talked about seeing other loved ones as well as beloved pets on the other side. As the months continued John became clearer about "life" on the other side. He talked freely about there being no pain, and only love over there. He spent a lot of time watching Pop fishing. One day he talked about God and I asked what does God look like and he said "amazing, awesome."

The hospice team loved coming to take care of Johnny. He talked freely about his experiences on the other side. He told everyone he was going to live with Pop but for some reason the house didn't have windows or a door. I understood this as a spirit message.

As the months went on the windows appeared and in August of 2012 he could now see the door. Of course we knew that this meant that Johnny's time with us was ending. We didn't know at the time the gift that Johnny would give us as he journeyed back into the world of spirit.

During the past seven months we had gotten used to Johnny talking about heaven and seeing those who had crossed over. Johnny hadn't been able to get out of bed physically the last four months of his life. That said, in thirty years I never heard him complain. His journeys into the astral planes of consciousness helped him find peace with the reality that he was leaving us. He loved looking at the pictures on the NASA site more than ever. He would marvel at the stars and say that's us.

Moving ahead to his last ten days of life in the physical, it was clear that Johnny was slowly disconnecting from those he loved. He was beginning to become weary that he could not figure out how to stay on the other side. He had slowly lost interest in food. Even his computer which he spent no less than 6 hours a day on was now being pushed aside.

He kept asking me why he couldn't just stay on the other side. As his journey into the light pulled him more and more toward the world of spirit Johnny began slowly to disconnect from us but he was clearly torn. He was not torn because he was afraid. He was torn because he knew we loved him. He was concerned what his physical death would do to me and to my husband Allan.

On August 10th through a nursing mistake Johnny's morphine pump had not been turned on. This led him into morphine withdrawal. The side effects were horrible and I knew deep within my heart that Johnny would not recover from it. After eight hours of violent sneezing followed by vomiting a nurse arrived at 5:00AM and gave him a shot. The vomiting stopped. He was weak and exhausted. At this point we still had no idea that his morphine pump was not working.

Sunday Morning August 12th one by one they came, my children, grandchildren and my mother came to see Johnny. It appeared that this was it. Johnny was leaving us. The weekend of diarrhea and vomiting had taken its toll. There was no way his heart could come back from this experience.

Another nurse came at 12:00 PM and told us he was now on comfort care measures. At this point we had figured out that he had been without morphine for forty-eight hours. From this point on John only had liquids; he had already stopped eating most solid food the week before. As the day went on, Johnny started looking a little better. I remember thinking, "Maybe, just maybe, we will have more time with Johnny."

On August 13th I could see that this was no dress rehearsal. Johnny was going to be birthing into spirit. During this time we gathered around him and supported his journey as we had always done. I began blogging on Facebook for friends and family so they could be a part of the final days of Johnny.

I now share our journey as Johnny birthed into spirit.

August 13th

4:00 AM Facebook Post: Call me crazy but I think Johnny is the cat with nine lives. Okay, maybe we have used seven of them. Right now he doesn't feel like he's going to cross over. His pain is under control. His fever seems to have subsided and his breathing is much better.

What a roller coaster ride this is of emotions. Yesterday watching my beautiful children and grandchildren by his bedside was a holy and beautiful experience.

Johnny came into this world and was an orphan boy. He is an orphan no longer. Johnny is loved. We cherish every moment we have with him. The love between him and Allan is beautiful to watch as well. They have such a beautiful connection of love.

Of course I can't forget my sister Sara and the ice. I think that's what helped. LOL. Sara kept feeding Johnny ice all day Sunday.

Whatever happens in the future yesterday was a day of love. Johnny knows he is loved. For now he sleeps. He is at peace. The room is filled with those who have crossed over. The angels are here. I feel peace and I will cherish it always.

Blessing One: Family, I have always believed the death of a loved one brings the best and the worst out in families. In our family it brings out the best. Johnny is deeply loved.

August 14th

It is 4:00 AM and Johnny is talking about the other side again. During his transition back into spirit Johnny spoke unencumbered by his speech. The words just flowed, especially after he comes back from the other side. He started talking about God yesterday as his eyes looked toward the ceiling. I asked him what he was seeing and he said "God."

Now in the early hours of the morning he has come back from the other side and this time he told me that God is everywhere. He said, "God is All-powerful, beautiful and is an Essence." He also told me that, "God is shining through daddy and daddy is God." He said, "very hard to explain, much to tell but can't explain."

He said he feels like he is on a tour. Johnny said, "The colors are awesome and are flowing through him." I asked him, "What do the colors feels like"? He said, "Hard to describe, but colors feel peaceful, serene and warm." He said, "God is the colors. God is everything. God is soon ready for me to come home. It just happens, the colors. God. Ahhh it just happens. Heaven's not a place." he said, "It just is. Heaven is God." Johnny was clear, he said, "I'm going home to be in God."

Johnny said, "Everybody has God in them but we have to decide how much of God we let other people see." I kiddingly said. "So I'm talking to God," and he said, "Yes, and so am I."

He said, "Everyone experiences God through one another, there is only God." I asked him "but what is God?" He said, "God is love. God is everything. God is home."

Johnny said, "God told me that when the time is right I will leave my body and I will become." Johnny had a hard time coming up with the words. He suddenly had a huge smile on his face and closed his eyes. He smiled and said, "I will become."

It is very peaceful in his room. Wow what an experience.

Blessing Two: How much of God do you allow others to see in you? Johnny's blessing for this day was so clear. He said that each one of us had to decide how much of God we would let others see shining through us.

August 15th

I have always believed in conscious dying. I call it birthing into spirit. The past few days have been, to say the least, emotional. Saying goodbye to someone you have journeyed with and loved for thirty years is hard. Saying goodbye to someone who has loved you unconditionally seems impossible.

I observe myself saying the right words. I coach Johnny to follow the light. He calls it the "golden light of God". You can see the amazement and wonderment in his eyes as he gazes off into the heavens.

Yesterday afternoon he asked if I saw the light. Through his eyes I did. Johnny said, "The light was everywhere, and the light was God." He said, "There are souls everywhere."

His eyes were fixed on the ceiling. Days ago he said he saw only heaven.

Today has been a day of Johnny going back and forth. He is laboring, much like a mother giving birth. Johnny is birthing into spirit. How can we hold on to someone who is birthing into spirit? And yet we do, I do. The little girl in me screams as she knows this man who has covered her will be gone from her life.

The tears flow as I sit here and watch each labored breath. This is no dress rehearsal, it's really happening. Johnny is birthing into spirit and he will soon be gone from our physical sight. He will never be gone. He will forever be etched upon our hearts. He has blessed our lives. His laughter and his ability to love unconditionally have helped me grow into the woman I am today. Even now he continues to take care of us, reassuring us that he is going home, home to God.

This morning he told Allan and me that all of our souls are together. He said, "They are watching us, sending us rays of love from the world of spirit." He keeps taking Allan's hand reassuring him that everything will be alright.

Johnny told us he has been inside his room in dad's house in heaven. He told us he has a computer. He said if Pop can fish on the other side he can have a computer. Johnny said, "Everyone creates their own heaven."

Saying good-bye, it's something we will all have to do someday. For now I will do what I do best. I will hold sacred space for Johnny to birth into spirit. We will surround him with our love. We will let the love of God, the angels and souls welcome him home, to the world of spirit.

Blessing Three: Soul Love is everlasting.

August 16th

Johnny woke up after a good night's sleep. During the night I would wake up and watch him talking. He was still sleeping. He would smile and at times laugh. I was aware that he was happy and this happiness did not include me. I must admit I felt some sadness in my heart.

Johnny told me that, "Heaven is a place where our souls live." He said, "I'm confused because over there you think something and it happens." He asked "How do I keep coming back here?" Then he said, "time." I asked him what he meant and he said, "God told me the time I would stay home in the light." I asked, "So home is not here?" He said, "Both have been home but my true home is what we call heaven."

Then he said, "But what is heaven?" I asked him, "What do you mean?" and Johnny said, "Heaven is not physical, it is love. Everything in this place we call heaven is expanded."

He said, "Hundreds and thousands and billions of souls." He said there are reunions of souls. I said, "You mean like you and daddy meeting?" He said "Yes but more." I asked him, "What happens to the soul of someone like Hitler?" Johnny said, "Hitler the man is different from his soul." He said, "Our souls are not punished for what man does."

Johnny told me, "The souls of those harmed by the man known as Hitler comforted the soul of Hitler." He said, "They understand on the other side what we on earth don't understand, there is only love." "Where is God in all of this" I asked him? He smiled and said, "God is in the soul and God is in the man." Okay I asked him, "Are you telling me that if a man takes a gun and kills someone down here their souls are watching?" He said yes, "but not judging."

I asked him, "Is there sadness and emotions in heaven?" He said, "Only love." I asked him if there was time in heaven? He smiled and said, "Time is not a concern in heaven, there is no such thing as time." He said, "Time is eternal as are we."

"Okay, so tell me about religion" I asked him. He smiled that smile again and said, "There is no need for religion in heaven, only love." He said, "Religion is only found on earth because it helps people remember love."

I asked him how he feels about coming back and forth and he said "Confused, very confusing." He said, "I thought I was there, but I keep finding myself back here." He said, "When I find myself here again it takes me time to remember what is going on."

I asked him, "What do you need from us." He said "Love, same old thing you always did, love."

He said "Don't hang on to me, let me go." He said, "I have to let me go too." I said, "Wow so this is truly a dance of body, mind and soul." He said, "I am becoming more soul, less John."

Gift Four: More soul less John and letting go of the physical. Johnny was clear that we had to let him go but he also had to let go of us and his physical body.

August 17th

Johnny and I both had a peaceful night. He spent the evening last night, with Kourtney, Abbie and Kathy while I spent time with Allan. I have seen an all too familiar look in Allan's eyes over the past few days. Allan's first wife, Jane died about twenty years ago. This journey that Johnny is on is bringing it all back.

Last night Allan and I had a date night. We didn't go far but we spent time together downstairs. For those of you who don't know, Allan came into my life ten years ago. I had made a commitment thirty years ago to journey with Johnny. I never imagined that I would find a man who would love Johnny too, but find him I did. During these past ten years Johnny and Allan have formed a strong bond of love. Talk about a soul contract. During the past two years as Johnny's health has declined Allan took on the role of caregiver along with me. When I had clients to see it was Allan that attended to Johnny's needs.

And now, my beautiful husband is finding it hard to let go of his soul companion. As Johnny lingers between worlds

Allan and I both are processing a flood of emotions. A few months ago Allan assured Johnny that he would take care of me after he is gone. Over the past few days Johnny keeps reassuring Allan that everything will be alright.

I don't think Johnny can see the sadness in Allan's eyes. His physical sight has changed since Sunday. Somehow Johnny knows that Allan's heart is heavy. It's been humbling to watch the love grow between these two men, and now as they say good-bye my heart overflows with love for both of them.

Johnny keeps telling Allan and me that our souls are together, in God. He calls heaven God. Johnny told us that our souls are connected as one in God. He said, "All of our souls are connected as one being of love within God."

He has talked a lot about soul life on the other side. I won't go into it now but as always Johnny continues to teach and inspire, even as he works to birth into spirit.

On a lighter note, this morning when Johnny woke up he told us that his "computer has a damn kink in it, and he won't stay in God (heaven) until it's fixed." Yes, that's right. Johnny has a computer on the other side. He also said he can't figure out how to work his computer because everything works differently in heaven.

I have always said that people die the way they live. Johnny has lived a life of grace, and now grace is all around him. I sit, and I watch, I wait, and I wait, for that moment when the next labored breath doesn't come. He is laboring hard. I guess in some ways we all are.

Blessing Five: Hope The gift from Johnny today is hope. As he shares with us his experiences from the other side, I am filled with hope that we are indeed connected and will always be connected, as Johnny said, in God. I have believed in an afterlife but now Johnny continues to fill my heart with the richness of life after physical death.

August 18th

As I listen to Johnnie's labored breathing, there is a part of me that screams inside, "I can't do this. I can't say good-bye to Johnny." I am painfully aware that part of me, who is screaming, is a very young part of me. I use to nurture her with food. Actually what I did was shut her up. Food is not an option, nor is shutting her up. I must honor this part of me that is being torn apart with each labored breath and moan. I must honor that life without Johnny isn't something I'm ready for.

Who is ever ready to say good-bye, especially to someone who has graced them with unconditional love? I remember daddy saying, "If you could see where I'm going you would all want to go with me." Daddy said, he would like more time with all of you, but who doesn't? I am reminded that birthing into spirit is a journey. Birthing into spirit really is a lot like giving birth to a child. Sometimes the labor is long. When we are born we leave the astral planes of consciousness for the denseness of earth. When we die, a physical death, we return to the light. Letting go of the physical seems to be a journey most people struggle with.

Many people think I saved Johnny those many years ago, but truth is we saved each other. When we met, our souls knew that we had found someone who we had traveled together for lifetimes. Johnny and I knew without words that we had found a safe haven within each other. Our soul connection and our soul contract had brought us to this juncture.

In 1982 when we met, we had both experienced life events that had wounded us. But on that day in January, our souls knew something that would only reveal itself with time. We had come together on that cold January day two broken people, but found in each other a safe haven, someone who understood, without words that together we were safe.

Many things have changed since that day thirty years ago. One thing remains the same, the safety we experience in the presence of each other. And that is why my little girl screams inside. Who will hold space for me like Johnny has. My beautiful husband will try. Allan knows that he cannot fill the space of Johnny, no one can. Our soul connection is eternal. In my heart I know this. Even knowing that we are connected forever, I wonder what my life will be like without Johnny.

A few months ago Allan told Johnny that he would take care of me, after he is gone. Allan told Johnny he knew he would not be the ray of sunshine and joy that Johnny was, but that he would do his best. I know this is true.

So here I sit, and I wait. I wait for the unknown. I wait to see what my life will be like without Johnny, my earth angel. I wonder will he wake up this time? Will he open his eyes and smile? Is this the beginning of the end of our lives together this time on earth? I don›t know. What I do know is that we will be saying goodbye. Johnny keeps reassuring me these past few days that we will always be connected for we are in God.

The labored breathing and the deep moans continue. Right now, in this moment I feel peace. I know that I will have the strength to face this time with grace. The room is full of departed loved ones and angels. I take a deep breath and although my heart is heavy I smile, for I trust that our connection is everlasting.

Blessing Six: Strength and Courage to live life without Johnny.

August 18th

Kourtney and I went to get dinner for everyone. We left Kathy with Johnny. We were only gone for about twenty minutes but during that time Johnny had what we believe to be another heart episode. When we came into his room, my daughter Kathy looked in distress. She told us that almost as soon as we left Johnny started getting chills, his body started shaking and his breathing was fast and furious.

When I looked at Johnny I thought for sure he was dying. My granddaughter Kourtney who has been by Johnny's bedside these past few days knew what to do. We hit the bullet on his morphine pump and gave him a dose of medicine. The nurses had explained how and when to use the medicine. I called my husband Allan and my son. They came, one by one. My sister Sara walked in the room. I wondered, had she sensed that this was the time? We gathered around his bed and I said, we aren't going to call grandma. We were sure Johnny was transitioning.

My eleven year old grandson Hunter spoke up and said, "Grandma has the right to know that Johnny is dying. If she doesn't want to come that is her choice." Hunter said, "I will go and tell her." His mother went with him. My mom returned to the house with them. The energy in the room was one of deep sadness. We believed Johnny was leaving us in the physical. We gathered around his bed and I began coaching him to go into the light. We had been doing this before but this was no dress rehearsal. The tears flowed as we held space as a family for Johnny to do the labor of birthing into spirit.

I do not have the words that will express the emotions I was feeling. I do know that I felt so blessed to have all these beautiful people surrounding Johnny. We loved him deeply and as a friend of mine said, Johnny was the heart of our family. There was no fear in the room. Sadness, yes, grief, yes, but there was also a sense of peace. This beautiful being of light, known to us as Johnny Angel, was moving closer to the light, or as he called it, God. I knew God was with us all. I knew that in God there was only love.

Slowly Johnny's body came back into a relaxed rhythm and we realized that we would have more time with Johnny.

Everything I believed about God, soul and life was coming into alignment as I continued to coach Johnny through his process of birthing into spirit.

I was being challenged to the core of my being. I knew that it was Johnny's time to leave us in the physical. He was tired. His physical body was beginning to shut down. Knowing all of this did not stop me from wanting more time with this beautiful man I had known for thirty years.

I had to let go. Somewhere deep within my being I had to trust that what I taught was also how I lived. I believe it was on this day that I began fully accepting that Johnny was leaving us. He was going home to God. I had to prepare on a deeper level of my being to say goodbye to my beloved friend, soul companion and teacher.

Blessing Seven: Acceptance, and trusting that we would always be together in God.

August 20th

I have helped other people birth into spirit. Helping people birth into spirit is something I'm very good at. Telling

Johnny to go into the light and don't look back, is the hardest thing I've ever had to do. He is so weak. His breathing is labored and after his heart episode yesterday I wonder, what is keeping him here? His body is very weak, but his love for us is so strong. He doesn't even have the energy to eat a popsicle. His life force is leaving him. I opened his chakras and blessed his body. I knew we were nearing the end of this part of our journey. The room was filled with beings of light. I continued to tell Johnny to go into the light.

We have done everything we can to reassure Johnny that we would be alright. Although his voice was weak Johnny talked about the angels, he only saw God. He was at peace.

Blessing Eight: Holding space for Johnny to birth into spirit. We were all blessed to experience Johnny in the many stages of birthing into spirit.

August 21st

Here we sit, Johnny and me. His breath is labored and his moans continued. I know he's not in any physical pain. The moans seem to help him release energy. Between these labored breaths Johnny told me, that in God everyone knows and loves him. He said, "Here on earth many people who saw me here didn't know me, they didn't see me. Some people," he said, "Even looked through me." Johnny said, "In God we see one another, we really see one another."

I held his hand and I could see the angel of death was now in the room. I had seen this beautiful angel before but now

I knew it was here to take my beloved Johnny back home, into the light.

As he labored trying to catch his breath Johnny looked at me and a huge smile crossed his face. I asked him what he was seeing. He told me, "An angel, a beautiful angel." I said, "Yes, Johnny, it is an angel, the angel of death is here for you."

I had been seeing this beautiful angel for the past few days. During all of this I felt comforted by this beautiful angel. This angel who had come to light the way home for Johnny was also pouring its essence of angelic light through me. Through tears, I told him, "Go with the angel, Johnny, Go into the light." I told him, "I love you, Johnny, go, go into the light." He weakly said, as I held his hand, "I love you too."

Through tears I watched as Johnny's spirit left his body. I knew Johnny was going with the angel into the light. However his body had not shut down.

During the last 10 days the sparrows have come to Johnny's bird feeder outside his window. We had never had sparrows come to the feeder before or since Johnny's spirit left his body.

I looked up the meaning of the sparrow and I read that the sparrows were flying around the cross and come to people after a long suffering. These sparrows actually sit and look in the window. To be honest, before I read about the sparrows they were creeping me out.

I was then reminded of a hymn and I sang it to Johnny.

~HYMN: "HIS EYE IS ON THE SPARROW"--LYRICS
A few words from the song:
"I sing because I'm happy,
I sing because I'm free,
For His eye is on the sparrow,
And I know He watches me."

The sparrows left a few hours after Johnny saw the Angel of Death.

Little did I know that Johnny was not done teaching us. Although his spirit was free Johnny's body had not shut down. It was like a frantic racehorse that had no rider. His breathing was fast and furious. I thought at the time this would last for a short period of time. I had no idea what the next forty-eight hours would be like as Johnny's body tried to shut down.

Blessing Nine: Freedom from the physical and the angel of death comes to light the way for Johnny to return to God.

August 21st
My thoughts focused on what I need do to help Johnny's body shut down. I knew that Johnny's spirit had left his body. But why wouldn't his body shut down?

I wrote: Is this comfort care? This fear we have about ending someone's life early is immoral. This is not about soul, love or God but about human ego.

Why is it better to allow someone's lungs to fill up with fluid and have them coughing and gasping for breath than to increase the morphine where it will end his suffering? Where is the comfort in this? Do we value the physical body so much that we cannot see when it is time to let go? Johnny has let go of the physical body. I saw his spirit leave. What am I to learn from this, I asked myself?

Yes, I know there is the dance of soul and ego but it is not John's soul that clings to life. Johnny's spirit left his body yesterday. Can't the nurses see this? He is dying, nothing is going to change this, but we can change the way he dies. Is the same health care system that failed him in life, failing him in death?

I know euthanasia is not a popular subject. I support death with dignity. I believe that many people end their lives from fear. I do not support this. They fear they will be a burden to their family. They fear death will be too painful for their loved ones to watch. I believe the birthing into spirit process can be a time of grace. The dying process itself offers lessons to learn. The experiences we had with Johnny during the past seven months as he birthed into spirit have been a gift.

I sit and I question why am I allowing this to happen to Johnny? He has worked hard these past ten days to cross over. I saw his spirit leave his body. What am I to learn from this? What am I to do for Johnny? Why won't the doctor and hospice team help his body shut down?

Why, because we value life much more than health, dignity or anything else. Is this life? Is this what John would want for himself? Of course it isn't. Nor would he want this for me or anyone else. The nurses keep telling us that Johnny doesn't feel any pain. I know he isn't feeling pain because Johnny's spirit already left his body. His body is not shutting down easily.

Gone are the smiles, and words of love about the other side. Gone is the laughter. There is only labor, intense physical exhausting labor. We continue to hold space for Johnny. We tell him to go to the light, even though we know his spirit has left his body. I know these hospice nurses are dedicated people. I know they work hard to give comfort care. But when comfort care measures are not working why, why can't they find it within themselves to bring an end to what now appears to be suffering? Perhaps we are the ones suffering? How do we continue to hold space for the body of our beloved soul companion to shut down? Again, I question, what am I to learn from this?

Three hours later

John's nurse just left. They increased his morphine and a few other meds. I know this is hard on the nurses and Dr.H. She is a good doctor and has gone the extra mile for Johnny through the years. His nurse is doing what she has been taught to do, which in my opinion is not enough. They could end this now. Comfort care is over. We need to help Johnny's body shut down.

He is still laboring hard, but it is not as intense.

I have spent the last thirty years of my life fighting for Johnny. The first doctor I fought with was the head of brain surgery at Hershey Medical Center. That doctor saved his life when he was twenty-seven and then left him to waste away with a shunt that didn't work for seven years. Many people had the opportunity to help Johnny back then, but all they saw was a man with half a brain, they looked no closer than that.

Johnny told me yesterday that the souls in God (heaven) all see him. He said "Here many people didn't see him." Johnny said many even looked through him here. So my friends, how many times have you looked through someone and did not realize that this person had a life lesson, or a gift to give you?

There are many Johnny's that grace our lives. Their souls have taken on a life of teaching us. I wonder, how many people passed by Johnny thirty years ago and looked through him? I know he has a sister who hasn't seen him in thirty years. What an opportunity she missed.

I fought for surgery and later found a doctor in York who believed in God, not that he was God. The doctor in Hershey forgot that fact. When the doctor in York operated on John he said, "I can do so much with my hands, the rest is up to God."

So here I sit and I wonder, what must I do to fight for Johnny now? Have I done everything in my power to help him through these final days? Truthfully I don't have the answer for that. I do know that I continue to hold space for this beautiful being of light. I will sit here and listen to his moans and labored breathing. I will watch his body twitch out of control. I will hold space until his body shuts down.

5:30 PM

Here we sit, my two beautiful granddaughters listening to Johnny's moans and cries. His beautiful heart is beating hard. At times he cries out and we tell him to follow the angels even though we believe his spirit has already left his body. We continue to hold space and talk to Johnny. This is all so confusing. I have helped so many people cross into the light. What am I to learn from this?

I wonder what my girls are thinking. They are amazing, holding space for Johnny to birth into spirit. Kayla never the quiet one, keeps telling him to go into the light. Kourtney pushes the morphine button, and keeps watch over the meds. A part of me would like to shield them from this, but I know they want to be here. They are looking at their phones in between taking care of Johnny's needs. Life still goes on, as it should.

Kourtney has been amazing these past eleven days, taking care of Johnny. Feeding him and tending to his needs. I trust her to be with him more than anyone else. She is going to be an amazing nurse. I wonder how this experience will shape her nursing experience. Kourtney has been a seer since she could talk. She also knew she was going to be a nurse since she knew what the word meant. Kourtney is eighteen and is now in nursing school.

Right now I feel peace. I have felt the love and support from my family, friends and students. I thank each one of you for the love and energy.

August 22nd

It is 1:43 AM I find myself taking care of the needs of Johnny's physical body. I believe Johnny's soul essence is no longer housed within his physical body.

I listen to his breathing, a sound I am sure will forever be with me. His breathing sounds like someone who is drowning in the fluid that has built up in his chest. This has gone on for well over twelve hours now.

I sit here with a timer on my lap going off every fifteen minutes, telling me it is time to hit the button on his morphine pump. I wonder why his doctor and nurses insist on keeping his body alive. What purpose does it serve? They carefully calculate the dose of morphine that will try to keep him comfortable. It is not working, his body is in distress. They make sure they don't over medicate him.

They keep saying Johnny will leave when he is ready. I have news for them: he has left. Other than the awful sound he is making Johnny has not moved his body with the exception of the breathing movements and twitching of his body. When I hold his hand there is no response. Again, I know that the beautiful being of light known to me as Johnny has vacated the physical body. When I reassure him that I am here, I am aware I do this more for myself than for him.

I will continue to hold space for Johnny, however I will not be telling him to go home to God for I know he has already done so. I believe yesterday morning when I saw the amazed look in his eyes as he saw the angel of death, the essence of Johnny left his physical body. His soul has no need to experience the shutting down of his body.

In writing that last statement I realized how this sounds. You see I believe just as many souls do not enter the body until after birth, many souls leave the body anytime along this process we call dying. Of course they hover around with love for the body which has been the home for the soul during this incarnation.

In the still of the night I feel John's soul in this room, as well as other souls and angels.

If I could draw I would draw a picture of the loving souls surrounding Johnnie's bed, along with angels of light. They are holding space, as I am, for this beautiful body to shut down. Then and only then will Johnny's soul be free. I feel covered by the angels and souls. I am very aware of being engulfed with love.

Even though I believe that the essence or spirit of John has left his body I find I cannot fully grieve until his physical body shuts down. I continue to do what I am told is comfort care, tending to the needs of his body until it takes its last breath. I continue to hold space for my beloved Johnny as his body slowly shuts down.

5:25 AM

For the past two hours Johnny's beautiful heart has been beating out of his chest and he is now in a rhythmic sound known as the death rattle.

I sit here and hold his hand. I have held this hand for many years and I know with a certainty that Johnny's spirit has left his body. No need for the drugs, other than the morphine. His body is beyond the need for drugs.

Occasionally there is silence and I wonder, "Is it over?" But quickly the silence is replaced with the sound I will forever remember.

At times I cry. The enlightened part of me reminds myself that Johnny is at peace. This is his body shutting down. The enlightened part of me feels and sees the angels and souls everywhere. The tears they will come, the sadness will be felt in the days and weeks ahead, for I am losing a part of me. My life will be very different. For 30 years I have held space for John as he has for me. I wonder, how will this void be filled? How many times will I wake in the night thinking I hear the ringer telling me that he needs me?

Lyrics for a song from "Wicked" express my journey with John Guy Baublitz III

"I've heard it said that people come into our lives for a reason.

Bringing something we must learn
And we are led
to those Who help us grow
If we let them
And we help them in return

I know I'm who I am today
Because I knew you"

This beautiful being of light has taught me, loved me and helped make me who I am today. I know with everything in my being that because two souls connected thirty years ago both of our lives were changed for the better.

Johnny's nurse came to see him around 11:30 AM. She was going to increase the morphine once again. After calculating the amount of morphine he took in over night she called the doctor. His breathing was fast and labored. He had been breathing the death rattle since 2:00AM. I didn't sleep more than ten minutes here or there because every fifteen minutes the alarm on my phone went off so he could receive the extra morphine.

As I heard John's nurse talking to his doctor I felt the anger rise.

Johnny's body was experiencing anything but comfort care. When I heard the nurse say "Yes, we wouldn't want to give him that amount of morphine because we could be giving him an overdose." She talked a little longer and they agreed upon the amount of morphine. When she hung up I said, "I can't believe what I just heard. Johnnie's body is experiencing anything but comfort care and you worry about giving him an overdose."

I said, "He's dying, why won't you help him?" She got very upset and said, "What you are asking me to do is illegal." I said, "You and I both know people practice euthanasia in the U.S. everyday." She said, "I will not do anything illegal." I said, "You would rather do something immoral than illegal." Then I began to cry. I told her, "For thirty years I have protected this man from doctors, nurses and others who did not see him. I have protected him and covered him and now I feel like I am letting him down." I said, "What is going on here is wrong."

His nurse said I could complain to her supervisor. We both took a deep breath and I told her I know she is doing her job, but her job is to give comfort care and she was not doing that. She told me if the increase of morphine did not help to call the hospice at 2:00. She said they would call the doctor then to see if she would raise the morphine.

The next two hours Johnny's body continued to race out of control. I will never forget the sound. At 2:00 I called the hospice. They said they would call the doctor. By 3:00 we hadn't heard anything so I called back. I was told the doctor increased the morphine. I was told it took so long to get back to me because they wanted to have their T's crossed and I's dotted. At 4:00 the nurse arrived. She was visually upset that Johnny's body was going through this. (tears) I told her, "You should have been watching this for the past thirty-six hours." She asked me if I had talked to his doctor and I told her not since last night. She said the doctor should see what is happening.

The nurse changed the morphine pack and again we continued hitting the bullet. This is what they call giving a dose of morphine every fifteen minutes. Again it didn't help. Around 6:00 I went downstairs to get some rest. I knew it was going to be another long night.

Around 7:00 I received a text from an angel and then a phone call from the same angel. She asked me how Johnny was doing and I told her his body was struggling and laboring hard. I told her I felt I was letting him down. I cried and told her this was inhuman and wrong. During my time at the hospice I had never seen anyone's body shut down like this.

I said if I knew how to help Johnny's body shut down I would do it. This beautiful angel of mercy told me what to do. She told me how to help Johnny's body shut down.

Allan and I walked the walk upstairs around 7:15. There was family in the room. We told them what we were going to do. My mother came in and gave him one last kiss and left. I kissed Johnny's cheek and told him I loved him. Allan held his hand. Our granddaughter Shae ran into the room and said, "My consciousness told me if I wanted to see Johnny one last time to come quick." We had wanted to protect her from this part of Johnny's body shutting down.

7:30 We gathered around Johnny's body which had been the vehicle for his soul's journey. We watched as his heart and breathing began to slow down. Gone were the torturous sounds. There was peace in the room once again. We listened to the music that Johnny loved. We continued to tell Johnny we loved him.

Slowly and peacefully his heart stopped beating and his body shut down at 8:07 PM. I realized as I held his hand that it felt no different after his physical death. I now knew without doubt that Johnny's spirit had indeed left his body thirty-six hours before his physical death.

Through tears I watched as Johnny's soul essence hovered around his lifeless body. I could feel his love as I watched him move into the light.

I cannot say I was ready to let Johnny go. Is one ever ready to let go of someone they have loved for thirty years? I do know that in the end I did what I have done for thirty years. I protected my Johnny. I did what I know was morally right and the loving thing to do. I would not, could not allow his body go through what it was going through. Even though I knew my sweet John's spirit was not in his body I knew that my sacred contract was not fulfilled until his body stopped breathing.

We called family and told them that Johnny's body had shut down. We spent an hour in the room before we called the nurses and undertaker. We all felt peace in the room despite what we had experienced the past thirty-six hours. Johnny was free. His body had shut down. He could now fully birth into sprit.

When the undertaker came to take Johnny's body away I must say I wasn't ready. I had never met the man and now I was supposed to hand Johnny's body over to him. I could see that he was a good man and I told him so. He asked me what I would have done had I not liked his energy. I told him I would have sent him on his way and called someone else. He told us to take our time with Johnny. When the time came for him to take Johnny's body I had to leave the room. My sister Sara was amazing and she stayed with Johnny's body until they took him away.

August 23rd 2012
Life Begins without Johnny

Here I sit alone in Johnny's room. As I cried, I allow the peace that is contained within this room to fill me up. During the past ten days Johnny reminded me many times that we are forever together in God. He said, "In God, all of our souls are one, and we will never be apart."

I once had a friend tell me that losing her brother was a painful experience. I do not believe grief has to be painful. What I feel is not pain. I feel, sad, empty at times, and uncertain about what life without John will be like. As a healer I have seen grief take people into the fire of despair and depression so deep they never allowed themselves to live again. I had one mother tell me,"I don't want to move on with my life, not without my son."

Move on I will do and so will John. Today he flies with angels and is engulfed with the love of God. He is in what he called, "The golden light of God." I believe that John was an angel among us. I also believe in this life he has earned his archangel wings. I will allow his soul to comfort me. I will embrace our soul love, for I know in soul we are together.

This does not mean I won't grieve, of course I am grieving. I will embrace my times of tears and sadness but I will also go on with my life, a life without Johnny. (deep crying)

For now, we go our separate ways, for I have a life in the physical to live and John has returned to soul life. I am comforted by the truth of our dual existence. I know we are connected as one within God.

In the days, weeks, months and years that I have here on earth I will embrace my future with the energy of my seeker. For today a new journey begins. I will seek to make sense of a life without Johnny. I will seek to embrace the love that is around me. I will seek to fill this huge void in my life with something that will honor the years I spent with Johnny.

I know within the core of my being that my years with John have prepared me for what lies ahead. I must admit at this moment I am looking forward with a sense of peace. I know that wherever my journey takes me, the soul known to me as John Guy Baublitz III will be my companion and guide. Is he gone from my physical life, yes, but he is not gone.

The laughter, love and joy that were Johnny will always be with me. I will not allow this grief that I feel to define me or our time together. I will do what Johnny did so well. I will live and embrace each moment of my journey here on earth as the gift it is.

To Johnny, my soul companion, husband, teacher, friend, guide and angel, I will miss you. I will honor your life by seeking to discover who I am without you as my constant earth companion. Allan and I will comfort each other, we will comfort our family. We will all walk together, knowing that in God our souls are forever connected. Our souls chose well when they chose each other.

Enjoy life on the other side. You have earned a long rest. Rest in the golden light of God sweet John, rest and know that "I am who I am today because I knew you."

May 2nd 2014

It has been an experience writing Johnny's story. I knew someday I would write about his birthing into spirit in a book. It's been twenty months since Johnny went home to the world of spirit. I must admit I have never read what I wrote during those ten days of grace. Reading the words that Johnny shared during his birthing into spirit I realize the gifts he gave us. Johnny's words were clear. He had no fear of leaving his physical body.

He loved us deeply and as he said we had to let him go, and he had to let go. Letting go has been hard. It was months before any of us felt his presence after he fully birthed into spirit. His essence was always one of love, but now it's even more consuming. He continues to teach me from his new home within God. I experience John's soul's essence as one would experience an ascended being.

I knew that my life with Johnny had prepared me for the next part of my soul journey. I was correct. What I learned about myself and what I loved about love has brought me to this place and writing my books. As I type these words I feel the presence of John and he is accompanied by angels. I know he is supporting my work and my life. I have peace knowing that John is home in God.

I will dedicate my life to educating people that we need to do more to ensure that the physical body of those birthing into spirit receives help in shutting down with grace. The journey of the incarnated soul is an amazing journey; one which need not end the way Johnny's did.

Johnny's gifts and teachings were many. He birthed into spirit the way he lived. He was amazing. He knew without question that he was going home to God. His traveling back and forth and sharing his insight will touch everyone who reads his story, I this I have no doubt.

I believe Johnny's story is not complete unless we talk about how the laws concerning death with dignity prevented John from having a "good death". There was no dignity or grace in the way the medical team allowed Johnny's body to go through what it did. There was no compassion, and no grace. I'm sure Johnny is not a rare example of the way the human body shuts down. We must change the laws and we must stand up for the rights of the dying. We must stand together to ensure that people are cared for and loved as they leave the physical life. We are incarnated souls. Honoring the journey of the soul includes honoring the physical body which was the home for the spark of God. There was no honor in the way Johnny's body shut down. There was no grace. I believe we must use what happened to Johnny to bring a consciousness shift in regards to death with medical assistance.

On a light note; Johnny continues to surround us with his love. His soul essence continues to pour its light upon our family. We are blessed. We know through Creator God and in Creator God we are forever connected. Souls, united forever.

CHAPTER SEVEN

WINDOW OF OPPORTUNITY

When I was a little girl it was clear my sister Debbie and I had a special bond. This bond would play out many times during our lives. When Debbie received her first diagnosis of cancer, our bond took us on a path that neither one of us could foresee. My older sister Debbie always seemed so strong, but during her twenties she began having health issues, and in her fifties she was diagnosed with cancer. At the time I was an energy practitioner, so I began giving Debbie sessions. Her prognosis was poor but Debbie's will was strong and her faith was even stronger. One day after I had given her an energy session, Debbie asked me to promise her that if she ever needed me to, I would support her choices. She also had me promise that if asked to do so, I would help her die if the time came.

Debbie knew that I believed in conscious dying. Debbie knew that I believed in the rights of people to die with dignity. We had several conversations about conscious dying. I explained to her that I believed in one's right to die with dignity. I explained to Debbie the months, weeks and days before birthing into spirit can be an amazing journey for everyone involved. We had had many discussions and she made her wishes known to me. Fortunately Debbie defied the odds and, although the cancer treatments left her body in a weakened state, she enjoyed about ten more years of life before my promise would be put to the test.

In the year 2012 Debbie was diagnosed with throat cancer. Once again she was given a dire health prognosis. Her options were limited and did not promise much hope of recovery. Debbie once again used her faith, humor and her strong will to get her through the cancer treatments. I must admit I did not support her chosen treatment choices. Debbie quickly submitted to radiation and chemotherapy after the doctor told her she would have a painful bleed out death if she didn't do the course of recommended treatment.

Somehow Debbie survived the intensive cancer treatment, but we could all see her body and her spirit were growing weaker. During this time I had my own life challenges due to the declining health of a beloved soul companion. Johnny transitioned in August and in October my sister Debbie came to stay with me for a few weeks. Our goal was to rebuild her body. During this time it was clear our roles had changed. Debbie was still the older sister but now I was the one she looked to for help and support. My sister was tired. Her body was weakened by the cancer treatment and, although her faith was strong, she had little hope of her energy level returning to anything that would resemble a vibrant life.

One day she told me that she wanted a better life for her husband Carl. He had been by her side during the cancer treatments. Carl was Debbie's primary caregiver. Carl tried his best but Debbie could see he was exhausted. Debbie was exhausted as well. After a few weeks Debbie went home and was focused on getting liquid health into her body. She had to receive all her food through a feeding tube. As I think back on those days I will always cherish our talks and hope we had about her beating the grim odds of the doctor.

By December it looked like Debbie was regaining her health, but the health challenges now shifted to her heart and congestive heart failure. She was in the hospital over Christmas. On New Year's Eve, Debbie was still weak but attended a traditional New Year's Eve bowling celebration. Although frail and weak she enjoyed the evening surrounded by loved ones. Little did anyone know it would be the last chance anyone would have to celebrate in this way with Debbie.

On January 6th I received a phone call from Debbie, one which is ingrained in my memory forever. She told me, "I'm in the hospital again. They are going to do a simple surgery to remove fluid from around my heart." Debbie assured me the doctors felt it was an easy surgery and after a few days in the hospital she would be able to go home.

After ending the call I looked at my husband Allan and said, "Debbie has a window of opportunity, and she's going to take it." I cried, my heart still feeling the loss of my beloved Johnny. I was not ready for yet another loss.

I knew that Debbie's transitioning would leave a void in my life and the lives of those who loved her. I have been asked if I don't grieve when someone transitions because I still have a connection with them and believe in an afterlife. Truth is, when someone dies, although it is only a physical death of the body, I for one miss the sound of the voice, the touch, the laughter, the physical presence in my life.

So on this January night I prepared myself for my beautiful sister choosing to leave the physical life we shared on the earth planes of consciousness. I must admit I don't think anything could have prepared me for the events which would unfold during the next few days. I am sure that our souls agreed before incarnating that if Debbie's life took this path I would be there to do as she had asked me years earlier, make the hard choices.

Around 11:00pm Debbie's husband Carl called and said the surgery went well. He told me the doctor had put her on a respirator and would take her off of it tomorrow. I had briefly questioned why the respirator was needed, but Carl didn't have the answers. The next morning my mother and

I went to the hospital. They were keeping Debbie sedated and still had her on the respirator.

I questioned why the need for the respirator. I was told it was a temporary measure. Her son decided to stay there that evening and since Debbie was sedated we went home. The next morning around 5:00AM I received a text from Dennis, Debbie's son. He said Debbie was awake and could communicate by writing. She wrote on a piece of paper, "SOS Katye come quick".

When I walked into the hospital room Debbie was indeed alert and clear. She reached for the breathing tube and shook her head no. She was clear she wanted off the breathing tube. I explained that it was temporary and told her I would find a doctor to talk to. When I talked to the doctor, he told me that they were trying to figure out what was going on with Debbie. It seemed like the simple surgery, which according to the doctor went well, somehow opened the flood gates and my sister's body was shutting down. The doctor was clear the breathing tube was keeping Debbie alive. Debbie was clear she wanted the breathing tube taken out.

Taking a deep breath after talking to the doctor, I now had to explain to Debbie and her family what was going on. I explained to Debbie the doctors needed time to try to figure out why her body was shutting down. The doctor told me they took blood samples and they would need forty-eight hours until they received the results. Debbie nodded okay but made it clear she wanted the breathing tube out. I promised her I would continue to do what I had agreed to do ten years earlier. I would support her choices and I would ask the questions no one else would ask.

As I watched her husband Carl and sons Denny and Kenny I could not help but think what was going through their minds. My nephews stayed by their mother's side during the next twenty hours, praying for a miracle I'm sure. I did what I could do to help them prepare for what was surely going to be one of the hardest experiences of their life.

I continued to talk to the doctors and we planned a meeting on Thursday. Carl, Ken, Dennis and I had several conversations about how we knew what Debbie wanted which was to be removed from the respirator. I knew the boys were feeling stress about the decisions they would need to make. Debbie's grandchildren came in to say their goodbyes. As Thursday grew closer it was clear to everyone the fifteen plus bottles and bags of medicines were keeping Debbie's body alive. Debbie spent most of her time sleeping but during periods of awake time she continued to make it clear she wanted off the respirator. She clearly understood that it was keeping her alive.

I know that Debbie was going between planes of consciousness during her sleep time. Debbie came to me during my own sleep time and assured me she was ready to transition. I had no doubts. I knew my sister was ready to birth back into spirit.

When Thursday morning arrived, I went to the hospital early. Her sons went to get some breakfast. I took my sister's hand and I told her that today we would meet with the doctors, and most likely the breathing tube would be removed later in the day. I then sang the song she sang during her cancer treatment, "This Little Light of Mine." Even though my sister had a breathing tube in, she sang it with me, her mouth moving with every word.

I remember holding the tears back. I knew that in the next few hours my sister would be birthing into spirit and my heart was heavy. I also knew Debbie needed me to be strong.

Our meeting with the doctors and medical team was to be at 10:00AM. Her sons, husband, my daughter Kathy and I were standing around her bed when the surgeon came in. He looked at the machine with the vitals and said, "Everything looks good. I will be signing off her case now." I asked him, "You do know we are meeting with the doctors to discuss taking Debbie off the breathing tube." He said, "They don't need me at that meeting. My job is finished."

At that moment the anger that I felt toward that man was almost overwhelming. During the sixty-four hours since Debbie's surgery, he kept telling us that the surgery was successful. The doctor told us he did everything right. My sister was dying and this doctor continued to deny what we knew. I believe he is an example of doctors not being in reality. Yes, his job was done, but it didn't change the fact that my sister was dying.

When he left the room, I asked the nurse what the hell was that all about. Denny looked at me and said, maybe mom is getting better. Maybe we should keep her on life support. I motioned for him to go out in the hall and said a few choice words about the doctor. I explained the doctor was in his own world, and when we had our appointment at 10:00 he could ask any questions he had.

The doctors, nurse and the palliative care staff were amazing. They answered all the questions Debbie's family had. They also informed them that they didn't understand why Debbie wasn't in a coma because her body was producing ammonia. The boys said they had smelled something whenever the nurses moved Debbie. It was clear to everyone in the room that my sister's body was shutting down. The decision was made to take her off life support later in the day.

Walking back to her room her sons and husband all said they needed to be alone for a while. Her husband asked me if I would tell Debbie what had been decided.

I will never forget how I felt as I held my sister's hand and told her the breathing tube would be removed. I told her that mom would be coming in to say goodbye. She shook her head no. I knew she wanted to protect mom, but I told Debbie mom needed to see her one last time. A tear fell from my sister's eye.

I talked to Debbie how proud I was of her and that I knew how hard she had fought during her last cancer treatments. I told her she now needed to shift her focus and begin the process of birthing into spirit. I knew that Debbie had already been shifting her focus into crossing over during her sleep time. I was sure her soul and angels had been communicating with her during her sleep time.

One by one her boys and husband came back into the room. Each one of us took the time we needed to thank her for being in our lives. I had explained to everyone that it would help Debbie if they told her that they understood that she was going back into the light. I watched feeling helpless as my daughter Kathy and her cousins tried to remain strong. Denny and my daughter Kathy had a special bond. Debbie and I gave birth to them in the same hospital that Debbie was now dying in. Debbie was like a second mother to Kathy so I knew she too was feeling many different emotions.

At 1:00 my sister Sara brought mom to say her goodbyes. Watching mom talking to Debbie was emotional for everyone in the room. Mom held Debbie's hand as she told her how much she loved her. She stood up and kissed Debbie's cheek. My daughter Kathy was taking my mom home so she too said her final goodbyes. Carl walked with them to the car and I can only imagine the conversation between them. As they left the room once again I saw a tear flow from my sister's eye.

After mom left, the palliative care nurse came in the room and explained they would take the tube out when we were ready. Ready, is one ever ready to take a loved one off life support? Is one ever ready to say good-bye to a wife, daughter, mother, aunt, sister or beloved friend? Ready, when were we ready? Never is anyone ready, but we knew what we had to do and we were all clear Debbie did not want the breathing tube. Debbie was ready.

Everyone had taken time to have their own goodbyes with Debbie. I remember my sister Sara telling me that I needed to let myself be a sister. I knew what she meant but I told her that Debbie didn't need me as her sister right now she needed me to be her birthing into spirit coach.

When it was time to remove the breathing tube everyone left the room but the nurse, palliative care woman and me. I held Debbie's hand as they removed the breathing tube and all the lines of medicines which were keeping my sister alive. The doctors explained earlier in the day it could be a few hours before Debbie's body shut down after they removed the breathing tube.

Surrounded by her beloved husband, sons, sisters and her minister Debbie began birthing into spirit. I sat down by her feet and told her to go into the light. As one who moves between planes of consciousness I could see the tunnel of light. I could also see the angels and beings of light who were in the room as well as the ones who were helping Debbie birth back into spirit.

I knew my sister Sara was supporting Carl and his sons so my focus was on helping Debbie go into the light. I spoke out loud so everyone could hear what Debbie was experiencing as she moved from this world to the next.

I remember at one point I could see Jesus at the other end of the tunnel of light. I asked Debbie, "Do you see Jesus?" She shook her head yes. I remember hearing her son Dennis say, "she sees Jesus, wow." As Debbie moved through the tunnel of light she kept looking backward, toward those of us she was leaving. I could see she was torn, wanting to leave, wanting to stay. I kept telling her to go into the light. I could see our father standing next to Jesus and I told Debbie I wasn't sure who was going to hug her first, daddy or Jesus.

As she moved deeper into the tunnel I could begin to feel the energy of spirit pulling her. This energy was compelling Debbie to leave the physical and return home to that which she came: the world of spirit.

Debbie looked back toward her loved ones who she was leaving one last time. I told her, "Debbie, don't look back anymore. Go into the light, let yourself go into the light, go, Debbie, be with Jesus, return to the light."

Suddenly, I could see Debbie surrounded by loved ones on the other side. As one journey ended for my sister, another one began. Debbie had returned to the world of spirit. When I returned my consciousness back into the hospital room, my sister Sara asked, "Is she dead?" I remember shaking my head yes, but I told everyone, "Do you feel the peace in this room? I want you to take it in, this feeling. Let yourself remember this moment in the weeks to come."

We were sad for our loss. Debbie however, was on the other side having joyous reunions with other souls. My sister, whose physical body was so frail and weak during the past few years, was now alive and vibrant in the astral planes. My beautiful sister had made the journey birthing back into spirit.

I told everyone, "Although Debbie's physical body was lying there lifeless, Debbie's soul essence still lingered around us." We sat there and I sang a song I knew Debbie liked as we allowed what had just taken place to flow into our awareness.

The hospital team was amazing and supportive during this entire experience. They had even told us that they don't see many families like ours. They told us most families' demand they do whatever they can as doctors and nurses to keep their loved ones alive. The palliative care person even asked me to come back at a later date to do an in-service about conscious dying and what I called birthing into spirit. I must admit I have not contacted them to do so.

One by one Debbie's husband and sons left the room. The minister had left first and I must admit I wondered what he had thought about what had just occurred. I'm sure nothing in his religion had prepared him for the experience he had just witnessed.

As I sat by Debbie's bed I looked at my sister Sara and said, now I can be a sister. For the first time since I walked into Debbie's room and realized she was indeed taking the window of opportunity to leave her physical body. I began to cry. I cried the tears for my sister I loved. I cried the tears of the little girl who wasn't ready to have her big sister leave. I cried for my sister who had lived and cherished every moment of her life and who left us way too soon.

Having a belief in the afterlife I knew I would see Debbie again. I knew our relationship would be different. Debbie would continue her journey in heaven. I would remain here on the earth planes of consciousness.

The nurse who had been with us the entire day told us to let her know when we were ready to have them take Debbie's body to the morgue. There was that word again, "ready".

I wasn't ready to have them take Debbie's body to the morgue. But I told her go ahead, do what you have to do. As I watched her take the many sensors from her lifeless body I couldn't help but think about my amazing sister. She had done everything within her power to fight the cancer that invaded her body. It was only a few weeks ago that she began eating solid food, her health was being restored, or so we thought.

None of us understood how tired Debbie was. She was tired of the physical pain. The medical treatments had left her emotionally exhausted as well. She didn't have it in her to cope with the heart issues that had begun to surface in the weeks preceding her death. She was clear she wanted her husband Carl to have a better life. I believe Debbie's faith in God and her love of Jesus gave her the courage to take the window of opportunity to shut her body down. The doctors with all their tests couldn't understand why her body was shutting down. They had even suggested an autopsy. When her husband Carl asked me about the autopsy I said Debbie had been poked and prodded enough during her life. Carl decided not to do the autopsy. I have wondered if Carl and his sons wonder, in the wee hours of the morning, what caused the death of Debbie. The surgeon was clear he had done everything right during surgery. The doctors were baffled and with all the tests, never figured out why Debbie's body shut down the way it did.

To me it was clear. Debbie was physically and emotionally exhausted. She chose to take the window of opportunity she was given with the surgery. She went home to the plane of consciousness within God that many call heaven. Debbie, my beautiful sister, died the way she had lived most of her life.

When she had a job to do she did it and she trusted that God would see her through. Debbie was fearless in life. Debbie embraced the death of her physical body as she embraced life. Debbie was ready to leave this plane of consciousness. Debbie died the way she lived surrounded by loves ones. She gave each one of us a gift even during those last final days and hours of her life. She made her transition, birthing back into spirit, with grace. Debbie was ready for the journey which awaited her in the place many call heaven. I know my beautiful sister who once graced our lives in the physical is still experiencing consciousness.

Was I ready to have her leave my life? No I wasn't, but I was ready for Debbie to be free of the pain she experienced as a part of her earth journey.

Debbie continued to come to me both in my dreams and waking state during the days and weeks following her transition. She knows I can see her and hear her, so she keeps popping in a lot and continues to do so. I remember about a month after she transitioned back into spirit she came to me, in waking state, with our brother Paul, who died at birth and our sister who died young. These souls have continued to grow. Debbie was happy to have us meet. I remember feeling a little jealous. They had a relationship with Debbie that I no longer had. Being multifaceted I do continue to have a relationship with Debbie. She is happy in the astral plane and has created her heaven. She is free and she is experiencing consciousness in the heaven of her creation.

My sister taught me many lessons. Her faith in Jesus and her love of life was a gift to everyone who knew her. She was not afraid of life. She lived life to the fullest. She took every opportunity she could to experience love. She shared her humor and her amazing gift of seeing the goodness in others.

When Debbie was given a window of opportunity to leave her physical body, Debbie was fearless. I believe Debbie's soul called her home. The grace she experienced during her life allowed her to birth into spirit when window of opportunity was given to her. I don't believe my sister gave up. She simply made a choice to leave the physical world. She wanted more for her husband, but I believe she wanted more for herself too. In her state of grace Debbie knew her physical death would not stop her from loving those she was leaving behind. Deep within Debbie, I know she was ready to embrace a new journey, one within God and one where she would continue to choose love.

CHAPTER EIGHT

PLEASE TELL MY STORY

As I was writing "Into the Light" I couldn't help but think of Magali. Her dying experience was very different from the other stories I have shared. I briefly thought about sharing her story, but decided not to. One morning, after writing I went into dream time. I found myself at a yoga studio. This other person, who seemed familiar, and I, were taking a class together. The yoga instructor gave us an exercise to do and I said, "I will never be able to do that." I heard a voice say, "Come on Kate you can do it." With excitement I realized it was Magali. Even in my dream, I could feel my excitement about seeing Magali. Since her death I hadn't seen or heard from her. And now here she was, in my dreams, as beautiful as she was in life. In my dream Magali asked me to tell her story. She said, "Katye please share my story, perhaps it will help someone else." She said, "I never found my way into acceptance. I was angry until I went to the other side."

Magali went on to tell me, in my dream, that since her physical death she needed to reflect on her life and her choices. She said, "Let me show you where I have been." Magali took me to a place that was isolated. She walked over to a beautiful stream. Magali said, "For now this is my heaven." She said, "The stream you see is from my country. It›s the stream I told you about."

I remember tears flowing from my eyes as I looked at Magali standing by her stream. She was beautiful. Her physical body which had been destroyed by the cancer treatments had died when Magali died a physical death. Magali now stood before me in her body of light, beautiful, peaceful and serene, asking me to tell her story. I agreed to do so. As I left her she thanked me for the love and kindness I had given her while she was alive.

As I moved back into waking state I was in awe of what had just occurred. Magali, beautiful Magali had just spoken to me in my dreams. Understanding that my experience with Magali was real I cried, because Magali had been very angry with me before she birthed back into spirit. Since her death I hadn't seen her in the astral planes of consciousness. What a gift Magali gave to me, coming to me in my dreams. I knew I would write her story. I believe her story will be a gift to many.

Magali was a student of our Two Year Energy Healing program. During that time I began to love Magali. She called me her spiritual mother. In January of 2012 Magali was diagnosed with stage four lymphoma. Her diagnosis was grim, but Magali was clear she could heal her body. She received standard medical treatment. Magali also received energy healing sessions four to five times a week and used food and herbs as a part of her healing plan.

During the six months of cancer treatment Magali looked at her life and her life choices. Magali always said she was selfish and put herself first. I told her that she was self-loving and putting herself first wasn't bad. Looking back I realize that Magali was right, she was selfish. Self-loving implies that we make our choices from our heart. Selfish implies we make our choices from a wounded ego. There was no doubt that Magali had a wounded ego and a very wounded little girl, one she had never healed.

During her healing from cancer Magali began to look at her childhood. As a little girl she was known as the daughter of the town whore. This left her with a huge wound. She left her country and came to America in search of freedom. She found that she could live in freedom but could never escape from the wounds of her childhood.

As she healed from cancer Magali began to radiate an essence of someone who knew peace. She believed she had finally healed the wounded little girl. Her body was healing, and so was her heart. In July of 2012 Magali was given wonderful news from her medical doctors, she was in remission. She had defied the odds. They wanted to keep a close eye on her and even suggested a few radiation treatments. This confused Magali because if she was healed, why would she need more medical treatments. She agreed to being monitored. She also agreed that if needed she would receive radiation at a later date.

Magali was excited about her healing. As her energy healer and teacher I advised Magali to continue working on her healing. She wanted to go home to her country she had left seventeen years earlier. Magali had only been back once since she had left. She wanted to go home and reconnect with family. She felt she felt she was emotionally strong enough. I remember telling Magali, "You need more time to heal. You are leaving your husband, son and your support team. When you return home your little girl will be put in the same energy you grew up in." I was clear, do not return to this place of your childhood. Magali was clear, I'm going. She promised to return back to the states in two weeks. I knew in my heart that Magali would not keep her word.

It would be 8 months before I spoke to Magali again. During those eight months Magali made choices which those of us who loved her did not agree with. During this time I also helped my sister and Johnny birth back into the light. I was drained emotionally. I continued to call Magali but she never returned my calls. Concerned I called her husband but he never returned my calls. I knew in my heart that Magali was making choices that would not promote health.

In March of 2013 I received a clear message from my guides to call Magali. They, the angels, told me she would answer the phone. Magali did indeed answer the phone and she started crying. Seems she had returned to the United States in January, but was too ashamed to reach out to her support group. The cancer had returned with a vengeance. By the time Magali came home she was a very sick woman. Her husband took her directly to the hospital. Three months later when I finally reconnected with Magali it was clear. The cancer was everywhere. She also had a huge tumor wrapped around her heart. Breathing was very difficult, and she looked like someone who was seven months pregnant.

I will never forget her words to me the first time we reconnected. She said, "The doctors have no hope. They have tried everything they know to do." She said, "You can heal me again, I know you can."

I reminded her the gift of healing the cancer came from her soul. Anna has taught me that disease is a sign that the personality is in need of soul realignment. Magali had received a healing those many months ago. By her choices, she did not go and change her life. Instead, she went home to her native country and made choices which were not in alignment with her soul. It was no coincidence that she now had a tumor around her heart.

It was clear the first time I saw Magali that the experimental cancer treatment had waged a war on her body. I told Magali we would focus on healing. Two other healers made weekly trips to the hospital which was over an hour away. It was clear to everyone Magali's body was not going to heal this time. I should say it was clear to everyone but Magali. Her husband held camp and stayed by her side, hoping Magali could heal. The hospital staff was clear. It was time to shift into hospice care. Magali did not accept this. She continued to believe she could heal.

The hospital gave us a form to fill out about what care measures she wanted. We also talked about her wishes for after death. Again Magali was clear. She wasn't dying. Her faithful husband was torn. Keeping the faith for healing and accepting what he was being told by the medical team was tearing him apart. Due to the change in prognosis, Magali had to leave the hospital. She had been there seven months. Her care plan had changed to hospice care. Magali never accepted this and was angry at everyone. Her anger toward me was clear. Why wouldn't I heal her? Of course I had never healed her the first time. Her healing came from within herself.

They transferred Magali to another hospital. The doctor at this hospital agreed to continue some kind of cancer treatment. Thinking back I remember how angry I was with the doctor who did her intake. He suggested when her body was stronger they could begin another experimental treatment. I asked him, don't you think you people have experimented enough. He said, "Magali wants to live. I am giving her treatment choices."

Magali did want to live, and she refused to talk about shifting her focus into birthing into spirit. Her anger toward the staff, her husband and me was clear. If we couldn't hold space for her physical healing, she wanted us to stay away. Emotionally, I was still missing Johnny and my sister Debbie. I took her anger personally although I knew it wasn't about me. The doctors told her husband insurance would not pay for any more medical interventions. Magali insisted the doctors continue to give her the cancer treatments. Now there was no choice.

Medical care shifted to comfort measures, but who would tell Magali? I told her husband I would try again to get her to understand that she needed to focus on birthing back into spirit. I told her she needed to allow her sixteen year old son to see her. She had kept him from seeing her because she wanted to protect him. She was angry. She told me to leave her room and just because the doctors and everyone else gave up on her didn't mean she was dying.

Her husband was going through his own roller coaster of emotions, including anger. He didn't understand why she had made the choices she did. Would Magali be dying now had she not gone home to her native country. He felt cheated of the time she could have shared with him and their son. He had tried everything within his power to help his wife live but now he was faced with the stark reality, his beloved Magali was dying.

Her husband and I kept in touch every day. I continued to help him find a place for hospice care. They moved Magali on a Friday afternoon in August. I went to the home to make sure that Magali would get the care she needed. The staff was wonderful. They were also aware of the needs of her husband. I had about two hours alone with Magali. She was nonresponsive but I knew she could hear me. I told her that I loved her but more than that God loved her. I told her to go into the light. I could see the angels all around her. I held her hand and thought she squeezed my hand. I felt some part of Magali could hear me.

I knew when I left the room that day that Magali was still not ready to leave those she loved. I wondered, as I left her room that day, would she find peace before she died. That was the last time I saw Magali until I saw her eight months later in my dreamtime. Since that dream, Magali has come to me and continued to ask me to tell her story. I believe her story would not be complete until I allowed Magali to tell her story she made her way back into spirit. I allowed Magali to magali told her story how

Here is Magali's story as she has told it to me from the other side, also known to many as Heaven.

Katye was correct I did not accept that I was dying. How could I accept that I was leaving my son Hunter and my husband Mitch? I had been so selfish and I was angry with myself. Choices. I hated hearing that word every time Katye said it. Choices. I made mine and now here I am dying.

I had wasted so much time trying to fight the cancer that I forgot what those around me were experiencing. Truth is, I didn't care. I cared only about myself and wanting to live. I wanted time to make different choices. Every time anyone tried to talk to me about dying I fought them.

When I realized that they were taking me to another place for hospice care, I still believed I wouldn't die. I remember being so angry that I even pushed away my angels. I pushed them away because they were no use to me if they couldn't help me heal.

Katye was right, I could hear her. Even though I was in this haze, I could hear her and others. I tried to let them know, but couldn't. I heard Katye telling me it was time to let go. How, Katye, I thought how can I let go? Katye kept telling me to go into the light. I didn't see any light. All I saw was darkness. Katye continued to encourage me to let go. "Go into the light," she said, but there was only darkness. I could see no light. Katye said, "Magali, let your angels help you go into the light. It's time, Magali, let go of the struggling and pain. Go into the light."

When a friend came into the room, I could see her, but suddenly I was aware that I was seeing her because I was standing next to her. I thought, "How could this be? My body is laying on the bed." I could see Katye and I could see she was doing her best to help me. When Mitch came into the room I went to him, but he couldn't see me. He was focused on my physical body. I realized no one could see me, not even Katye.

As Katye kissed my cheek one last time, I tried to get her attention. I thought she felt my presence, but she left the room. As I looked at her leaving, I realized that it would be the last time I would see my spiritual mother. She had taught me well. I looked at my physical body lying on the bed, I knew I finally had accepted that I was dying. I wasn't sure what to do and just as I thought this there they were, my angels. They were here to help me go home, home to heaven.

Everyone continued to focus on my physical form. As I continued to wonder what to do I began to feel the most amazing energy. This energy began to pull my body of light into a beautiful tunnel. There it was, just as Katye said it would be. I looked back at my husband and my body which was still alive. My angels assured me that I would see them both again.

Even though Katye wasn't there I could still hear her words echoing, go into the tunnel of light. As I moved into the tunnel of light, I was aware I being surrounded by angels. The swirling masses of colors were beautiful. The colors were flowing everywhere. I could hear music and I could still hear my husband and those in the room where my physical body lay. Again I could hear Katye telling me, "Don't look back Magali, go. Go into the light."

Suddenly I could hear nothing but the beautiful songs of angels. My light body was pulling my consciousness away from my physical body to another place. Surrounded by my angels, I made my way through the tunnel of light as I came out of the tunnel of light I realized I knew where

I was. Suddenly I felt an overpowering essence of love. I was home. Gone was the pain, the anger, the suffering. I was home in spirit.

It's hard to explain what my life has been like since I returned home to spirit. I still have consciousness, but it's different than on earth. I was taught that there was no such thing as time, except on earth. This is very true. I thought I had been in heaven a very long time. Through the screen of life events, I watched as my loved ones and my physical body had an ongoing experience. How could this be, I questioned. Am I not dead?

Through the screen of life I could see that my physical body was still shutting down. I had a choice to make. I could go back and participate in my physical death or I could stay in heaven. I chose to go back to earth but chose not to re-enter my physical body. Instead I tried as many who are transitioning do, to try and console my loved ones.

I watched as those around me cared for my physical body. I watched as my husband tried to remain brave. If only he could hear me. I tried to get him to hear that I was not in that physical body. Even as my body lay dying I was free, but those who loved me were not free. I realized my choices had caused pain to those who loved me.

It happened rather quickly, my physical death, that is. Once my spirit left my body, my body began to shut down. I watched as my body took its last labored breaths. I watched as my husband realized I was gone. He loved me. In fact he loved me more than I was capable of allowing anyone to love me. I knew he would take good care of our son. I questioned, at that time, if he would take good care of himself.

As my light essence moved back into the tunnel of light I knew I had more soul growth to do and much to learn from the choices my personality had made during my life as Magali. After I made my transition back into spirit I went into isolation. This was my choice. There were many in heaven who wanted to help me. I wanted to think about my choices I made on earth. For now, I have chosen not to have contact with those I journeyed with on earth. I knew I had a lot to understand and heal. Even in this place known to many as heaven, there is still soul growth and soul expansion to experience. We continue to grow and evolve after we have returned to this place many call heaven.

In heaven I now have a body of light. I still have consciousness, however I have no ego. In this place many call heaven I am learning and continue to view my life choices. I do so from a place of non-judgment. In this place of love I look at my soul contracts and the plan my soul had for my life.

I made my consciousness known to Katye at this time because I wanted her to tell my story. I wanted an opportunity to share what I now understand that I didn't understand on earth. There never seemed to be enough love when I was living on earth. I always wanted more, more love, more joy, more. I also always did what I wanted with little thought to how my choices affected others. Now, in this place of spirit I understand how my choices affected others. In fact, I now understand that my choices I made while alive continue to affect those who loved me.

From this place of non-judgment I understand that on earth because of this thing we call time I wasted opportunities to experience love. Regrets, from this place we have no regrets but I can learn from my earth journey. When I'm ready to help those who are experiencing pain and sadness from my choices, I will shift my consciousness to helping them move on. I want them to move on and create a life of love without me. I know it will be their choice to allow this or not. I will begin by connecting with them in their dreamtime, as I did with Katye. I will show them my little piece of heaven.

For now I leave you with these words. Move away from the childhood wounds. Do not allow the wounds from childhood to define you. Look for pain, sadness and despair, you will find it. Look for love, joy and peace you will find it. I did not understand that I was loved and that I was love. I know today that I am love and I know that I was loved. Enjoy your life and be self-loving. When you love yourself completely, you cannot help but love others. It's truly all about love.

Magali's gift was learning to love one's self of and learning that letting go of the physical body is not the end of consciousness. We can learn a lot from Magali by listening to her words of love.

August 22nd 2014

Magali is another example of how the current healthcare system uses excessive measures. Magali's disease was beyond anything medical intervention could help. Still the doctors gave her experimental treatments and false hope. Instead of helping her face the hard truth that she was dying they were more than willing to continue treatments until they were forced to stop by her health insurance. During the weeks before she birthed into spirit I was the only one who tried to help her understand that the last few weeks of her life could be spent talking with her loved ones and finding closure not only for herself but her family. There are many like Magali out there needing someone to help them shift from fighting to live to birthing into spirit with grace. It can be done but we need healthcare systems and the laws to change. We also need a consciousness shift about physical death being a part of the journey of soul.

CHAPTER NINE

EMBRACING GRACE

It's amazing what we can learn about life from those who are birthing into spirit. If given the opportunity, they will share their experiences. The stories I have shared may seem unique but they are not. What was unique was the space created which opened the door for each person to share their experiences.

I have always believed one of my gifts is helping people birth back into spirit. I knew at the age of nine when my grandfathers died that those in my tribe had forgotten that death was not a bad thing. Slowly over time I grew to accept the beliefs of those around me. It would be many years later that I found myself beginning to advocate for people to understand that dying a physical death was a part of the journey of the incarnated soul. My life has been dedicated to waking people up and helping them live conscious soul inspired lives. Living a conscious soul inspired life, I believe, helps people to have a conscious soul inspired birthing into spirit experience.

In Chapter One we asked you to imagine a world where the process of dying is embraced as a part of the journey of the incarnated soul. We asked you to begin to understand that death is not an ending but a continuation of the journey of the soul. We shared our vision that someday birthing into spirit coaches will be trained in the future to support the process of those who are leaving the physical life and returning to spirit. We shared our vision that medical help would be available to ensure that the birthing into spirit process honors and helps the incarnated soul leaves the physical body with grace.

We need to begin creating a world where death with grace is not just a dream but a reality. The time is now. The process of dying a good death is as important as living a good life.

The question becomes, how do we create space for those who are birthing back into spirit? How do we create space in a world which has little understanding that we are incarnated souls and we are on a journey for soul growth and soul expansion?

I believe a consciousness shift must occur. I also believe that we cannot talk about birthing into spirit without talking about death with dignity. Talk of heaven, the afterlife and the journey of the incarnated soul must include a world where the dying process is supported by the laws of the land and the medical team of the one birthing into spirit.

When I wrote "Into the Light" I realize now I was not ready to deal with the subject of death with dignity. Death with dignity means many things to many people. To me death with dignity assures the person birthing back into spirit will not experience one moment much less thirty-six hours as Johnny's body did as it tried to shut down. Johnny's birthing into spirit journey was an amazing journey and as a family we were blessed. Unlike many families we talked openly about Johnny birthing into spirit. Johnny had no fear of, as he said, going home to God. We believe in an afterlife so when Johnny talked about heaven we easily supported his experiences. Our family was not afraid of death. Of course we were sad that Johnny was leaving our physical lives but we understand that he was tired and it was time to say good bye to our beloved soul companion. We had gathered together a great team of care givers, including his doctor. I was his birthing into spirit coach. We had all the bases covered or so we thought.

Nothing in my sixty years of life had prepared me for the way Johnny's physical body shut down. Elizebeth Kubler Ross got us talking about death and dying in the late sixties. Hospice care has given comfort to many. I wonder, "Are most families left to hold space for the actual process of dying like our family was: alone and feeling helpless?" Johnny's nurse did nothing to help his body shut down. His doctor did nothing to help his body shut down. Why? Because they said it was illegal to do so. My dad, David, had to starve himself to death.

Dad had lived a good life and believed being an old man in a rocking chair would be torture.

A life well lived need not end with a dying experience which does not honor the journey of the incarnated soul. Birthing into spirit is a conscious dying process that embraces every moment of life as one to be cherished including those leading up to physical death.

I value every moment of the journey of the incarnated soul. I value every human experience. The experience of birth, the first amazing sound of the infant child and every inconceivable experience until we birth back into spirit is a part of the grand journey of an incarnated soul; one which I value and hold sacred.

We place so much value on keeping the physical body alive that people are afraid to allow the dying process to unfold as a part of the journey of the soul. Pain management and comfort care is a small part of what people want when the end of life decisions need to be made. People want assurance that there will be someone there to help their physical body shut down. Sadly this is not the case.

The archaic laws which demand that caring professionals and family members stand by and do nothing to help the physical body shut down must be changed.

This is what those who live with a terminal illness want. They simply want to know that when there is no more will or fight to hold onto the physical body there will be someone who will help them birth into spirit and help their physical body shut down with grace.

If the person whose physical journey is ending cannot have confidence that the dying process itself will be one of grace it's very hard to focus on heaven or anything else. There are many movements today seeking the rights of people to die with dignity. This means many things to many people. A holistic approach would include the right of someone who is terminally ill to determine their end of life care, including the shutting down of the physical body.

Most people are uninformed about their healthcare. They are just as uniformed about the dying process. I know I had no idea that the caring people who took care of Johnny for seven months would stand by and do nothing to help his body shut down with grace. During the last thirty-six hours of Johnny's physical life our family was thrown into anger and feelings of helplessness. Not because Johnny was dying but because there was no medical help in shutting his physical body down.

I encourage everyone who reads this book to become informed of the laws in your state or country concerning death with dignity. Will you or your loved one be supported by the healthcare team as the stages of dying are experienced? Will you or a loved one be supported by the healthcare team when it becomes clear that the body is shutting down and physical death is imminent? Is your health care team trained in not only caring for the physical body but also the incarnated soul who is birthing into spirit?

Will they honor the experience of the journey of the incarnated soul as the birthing into spirit moves them away from physical consciousness into spiritual consciousness? Have they an understanding that the care of the person birthing into spirit must go way beyond just comfort care?

Once there is reassurance that there will be support in shutting the physical body down the focus can be placed on birthing into spirit and helping the personality have a good death.

Twenty-two years ago I read a book written by Elisabeth Kubler Ross. Her book, "On Death and Dying" gave us a better understanding of the stages that people who are terminally ill experience. She describes five stages people go through as they realize they are dying. The last stage is acceptance. Peace is often experienced for those who enter the stage of acceptance. What Elisabeth did not write about was where this stage of acceptance allowed the dying to go.

I believe we can add a sixth stage to her model of death and dying. This stage is grace. Accepting that physical life is ending opens one up to grace.

For people who reach the stage of grace, an amazing journey awaits them. The fighting, pleading, bargaining and anger are gone. With acceptance comes peace and with peace, grace is allowed to enter.

During stages five and six people begin to detach from the world around them. They do this, we think, because they are losing interest in life. I believe they do this not because they lose interest in life but because something is pulling them toward the light. They lose interest in the physical because the world of spirit is one's true home. Letting go of the physical body and loved ones is not easy, no matter what the beliefs are. The light of one's soul begins to pull them away from physical consciousness into spiritual consciousness.

Their physical senses that they primarily used during their earth journey begin to shift. They don't lose interest in food, they are simply being fed by spirit. They don't lose their eyesight, they now see clearly. Perhaps for the first time in their lives they see beyond the veil of physical consciousness. They see through the illusions of physical consciousness and see what has always been available to them. They see the world of spirit.

Angels, departed loved ones and heaven are seen as one connects with the world of spirit. If given the opportunity they will talk about what they are seeing. They don't lose their desire in being touched or touching, quite the contrary. Those who are birthing into spirit often experience touch as a distraction. As their sleep time takes on new meaning they begin experiencing this place we call heaven. They begin living in two planes of consciousness. Many people like Lana love being touched until their body shuts down. Each person birthing into spirit has different needs.

Those birthing into spirit do not lose their hearing, in fact the opposite is true. As one begins to shift into spiritual consciousness they now begin to connect with the stillness of the voice within them.

This voice was always there but physical consciousness often blocked this voice out. Now birthing into spirit the voice of one's soul is clearly heard. The clutter of life seems to fade away as one moves through the first five stages of Elisabeth's path as one births into spirit. Now the voice of spirit and the songs of angels begin to flow into one's consciousness as one enters this stage of grace.

Intuition becomes clear and the senses are heightened as those birthing into spirit enter the stage of grace. Intuition is the voice of one's soul. Our intuition, the voice of our soul can be a guiding force during our lives. The voice of one's soul is often crowded out by the clutter of one's everyday life. In the stage of grace, intuition and one's soul begin to move to the forefront of one's consciousness.

Do the dying need to disconnect from those they love? My experience has shown me no, they do not. Those who are birthing into spirit will continue to connect with loved ones if it doesn't distract them from moving into the light. Space is created for experiences which cannot be explained by physical consciousness.

Holding space for a loved one, birthing into spirit, honors that he or she will be spending more time in the world of spirit. Food, conversations, things which once interested them are cast aside as they birth into spirit.

We have gotten better at creating space for babies when they are born. In "Conscious Construction of the Soul" Anna offers us a vision of creating space for the birth of an infant. Anna said, "When a child is born, everyone in attendance should pause and honor that which has just taken place." A soul has incarnated into the physical. Anna explained that everyone who is in the room should honor, that no greater gift than this has ever been given. The gift is the experience of life. We honor labor. We honor the energy it takes for both mother and child as they experience the dance together. We rejoice when a child is born.

It's now time to honor death in the same way. The birthing back into spirit is tiresome at best. Personalities which have known life primarily through physical consciousness must now shift into leaving the physical body and letting go of the physical world. Letting go of relationships, wounds of childhood, and old outdated beliefs is a lifelong process.

People who share their experiences of moving into the light are labeled as delusional or drugged up. This way of thinking does not affirm the journey of the incarnated soul nor does it help to create space for birthing into spirit. Birthing into spirit can take one on an amazing journey as the dying shift from physical to spiritual consciousness.

We begin by allowing ourselves to connect with spiritual consciousness as we live our lives. I believe we can only create space for those birthing into spirit if we have embraced that we are spiritual beings.

We view death as final, as an ending when in truth it is another birth, another beginning. To help someone birth into spirit we must first deal with our own fears of death. We view death as taking someone away from us. In truth our loved ones are on their own path and joined with our lives for soul growth and soul expansion. We do not have ownership of our loved ones. We create space for those birthing into spirit by honoring the time we have had together. We create space by honoring the spark of Creator God which gives us life also continues even after physical death.

Elisabeth's first four stages of death and dying seem focused on physical consciousness. As one moves into the fifth stage of acceptance we can begin to offer those birthing into spirit and ourselves an opportunity to move into the sixth stage of grace.

People who have not lived a conscious life themselves find it difficult at best to support their loved one as they birth into spirit. As we shift our consciousness to be open to the possibility that physical death is not the end of consciousness we can begin to create space for those birthing into spirit. Just as we hold space for the incarnated soul who is born into the physical, we can begin to hold space for the incarnated soul who is birthing into spirit.

One must shift in consciousness to include that there is more to the birth, life and death cycle, much more, if one is to hold space for those birthing into spirit. Religion and science are often barriers where embracing that we are incarnated souls. Moving beyond religion and science and listening to those birthing into spirit opens one up to believing that heaven is real and physical death is a part of the journey of the soul. I believe by doing this many will begin to honor their own experiences with heaven and departed loved ones.

When we focus our consciousness on physical reality we live our lives in a vacuum of experiences which casts aside the sacred and mystical experiences. By shifting our consciousness away from physical consciousness, we will begin to acknowledge the experiences of those birthing into spirit. We begin to hold space for those birthing into spirit by understanding that only the physical body dies. This shift in consciousness allows us to embrace the reality that physical death does not end the journey of the soul.

Living a life of grace doesn't have to wait until one is dying. By embracing spiritual consciousness as we live our lives we can shift into a state of grace. Just as the dying experience heightened senses we too can experience an expanded state of consciousness throughout our lives. When we honor our own everyday mystical experiences as normal, we begin to honor that seeing departed loved ones and heaven is as real as any experience. With grace as our guiding force we live our lives with love. With grace as our guiding force we embrace the spirit within ourselves. With grace we honor that our true essence is spirit. With grace as our own guiding force, death is simply a part of a grand cycle of amazing experiences.

We are told that time is an illusion. If this is true could this explain how someone can die a physical death but still exist on another plane of consciousness, a place many call heaven? Could this explain how many of us still experience the presence of someone we loved who has died?

Physical consciousness often blocks experiences with those who are gone from our physical sight. We tell ourselves that the dreams we have where we are visiting our departed loved ones are just dreams. We tell ourselves when we smell the scent associated with a departed loved one that it's our imagination. Just as we deny the experiences of those dying we deny our own experiences of heaven.

To deny heaven is putting limits on Creator God. By opening one's consciousness to the world of spirit one creates a paradigm shift. The world as they know it is forever changed.

Is it possible that we have never left this place called heaven? Perhaps heaven is indeed not a place, but as Johnny said is God.

Lana was very clear that all we had was the eternal present moment. Could it be that in the eternal present moment there is only God, therefore death is an illusion?

Johnny told us that heaven wasn't a place, that heaven was God. He said that we are always together in God. Could it be that we do not die at all but simply by leaving the physical we awaken to that which we truly are, spirit?

David, my dad, told us that if we could see where he was going we would all want to go with him. Could it be this place called heaven is known to us even as we live on the earth planes of consciousness?

Magali, told us our journey is all about loving and being loved.

Can we believe the stories of Debbie, David, Sam, Magali, Lana and Johnny? Can we move past what we have been told about death and believe that there is a place called heaven and our loved ones still experience consciousness? I believe we can. I believe many will read the stories I have shared and will embrace that heaven is real and their loved ones still exist within God. Spiritual consciousness allows us to embrace that within Creator God there are many planes of consciousness. Physical life on earth is one of them. Spiritual life in the place many call heaven is another.

CHAPTER TEN

BIRTHING INTO SPIRIT

Consciousness is changing. Honoring that the creative force of the soul continues to experience consciousness after physical death, space is created for the birthing into spirit process.

Birthing into spirit is a conscious dying process. Birthing into spirit honors physical death as the ending of life on earth and embraces that consciousness continues after the death of the physical body.

Birthing into spirit embraces the sixth stage of dying, which is grace.

For those who reach the stage of grace, the experience of dying is a part of the journey of the incarnated soul. As the personality begins to let go of the physical, he or she embraces the world of spirit in new and wondrous ways. Letting go of the world around them is seen as the natural part of the process of birthing into spirit.

Changes in sight, taste, touch, hearing and intuition are honored. Understanding these changes are a part of the training for birthing into spirit coaches. Families are taught to understand these changes are not because their lived one is losing interest in life but because the world of spirit is calling them home.

Education about birthing into spirit needs to be taught to friends, family and caregivers. For this to occur the medical community itself must shift. Comfort care for the dying must include care of the incarnated soul who is birthing into spirit.

Education is needed within the medical community. Health care providers need to understand when it is time to stop unnecessary medical intervention and focus on comfort care. Sensitivity training is needed to help medical professions understand that patients are not delusional when they begin to see through spiritual consciousness.

Willingness to hear and talk about the experiences as one moves back and forth between heaven and earth is key to holding space for those birthing into spirit. Training for birthing into spirit coaches includes taking about death. Many people including healthcare workers waste time and energy by avoiding the subject of death.

Shifting to spiritual consciousness allows family, friends and caregivers, the opportunity to see dying as a part of the cycle of life.

Conversations about physical death and heaven are encouraged rather than avoided. Families are giving the opportunity to talk openly and freely as they support their loved one birthing into spirit.

Family, friends and caregivers can offer support by telling those who are birthing into spirit to go into the light. The light experienced by those who are birthing into spirit can become all consuming. If the personality has a strong religious connection encourage them to move into the light toward the chosen deity and or family who awaits them on the other side. My experience has been that those birthing into spirit often look back toward the loved ones they are leaving. Encourage them to continue moving into the light and not to look back.

Birthing into spirit is not a religious experience. Birthing into spirit honors and works with the beliefs of the person who is dying.

Hold space for those birthing into spirit by honoring that, although the physical journey is ending, a new journey awaits them.

The light of Creator God pulls those birthing into spirit. When one has fully shed the physical body, there is no death of the spirit. With physical death the spirit, that spark of God which resides in us all is free. Our spirit continues evolving and growing in consciousness in this place many call heaven.

If you are with someone when they have birthed into spirit allow yourself time with the departed loved one's physical body. Those who have crossed over into the light will often hover around the body they have just left. They are now in their body of light. They are not limited by time. Let yourself experience the peace in the room. Let yourself be open to the comfort from your own angels and those in spirit form.

The grand cycle of consciousness continues in this place many call heaven, for within Creator God there is only love.

CHAPTER ELEVEN

THIS THING CALLED GRIEF

In the hours, days, weeks and months after the death of a loved one they will often appear to you in your dreams. Grief often blocks out any messages and or experiences of our loved ones in heaven. As you create a life without your loved one, know that he or she continues to have consciousness. Everyone creates their own experience of heaven. The truth is, everyone creates their own experiences on the earth planes of consciousness. The world of spirit has no duality. Love is the foundation on which our departed loved ones build their own little piece of heaven.

Our departed loved ones will use dreamtime to show us their own little piece of heaven. You will often feel their presence. Honor these moments as real. Honor that your loved one is in heaven and is still experiencing consciousness. Embracing spiritual consciousness allows you to experience heaven and the world of spirit.

Honor your grief but do not mourn. Mourning does not allow us to move on with our lives. Mourning keeps us focused on the past which often includes regrets. Grief comes and goes like the tides of the ocean. Sometimes you will feel knocked down by your grief. The simplest memory of joy can take you into grief. Honor your grief. Those who have birthed into spirit fully understand that their loved ones have not fully embraced spiritual consciousness. They understand that on the earth planes of consciousness, this thing we call grief is needed by many. The limitations often imposed on them by an unconscious world cease to exist.

It is often very difficult to let go, for those of us who remain in the physical, after a loved one has birthed into spirit. When a loved one births into spirit our physical life has changed. There is often a huge hole in our lives in the space our loved one occupied. Letting go of dreams and plans we had with our loved one who has birthed into spirit becomes a part of our life lessons. Perhaps life is a dress rehearsal for when it is our time to let go and birth into spirit.

Even if you believe your loved one has birthed into spirit, most likely you will still experience grief. You have some conscious understanding that your loved one continues to experience consciousness in this place many call heaven but your life has changed. It is often that empty space within our life that we find ourselves grieving. Honor the journey you have shared with your loved one. Honor that your grief is about the void left in your life. Understand consciously that it's impossible to grieve for someone who has birthed into spirit. Your grief is about how your life will change because your loved one has left the world of the physical.

Within God there are many planes of consciousness, life on earth being one of them. Within God there is a place many call heaven. Our loved ones have shed the physical and now they are clothed in light. They live, they create, they grow, and they continue to love. They are on their own journey. The truth is that we are each on our own journey, we always have been.

Honoring that physical death is a return to spirit we can begin to honor what those birthing into spirit know. There is no death, only a change in consciousness. For those of us still experiencing consciousness primarily on earth we must build a life without our loved one. The guilt that many experience as they create a life without their loved one can be released. Guilt about moving on with one's life is wasted energy. As soon as someone has fully birthed into spirit they move on without those they left on earth. They have no guilt for in spirit, they know only love.

As we allow ourselves to move from grief, we begin to embrace grace. In this place of grace, death is no more, for death is an illusion.

Today, embrace spiritual consciousness. Today, invite grace to enter your life. Through grace embrace the truth that within Creator God we are always together. Within Creator God there is no death, consciousness continues, as does the journey of the soul.

ACKNOWLEDGMENTS

I want to acknowledge and thank Elisabeth Kubler Ross. From the moment I read her book *"On Death and Dying"* I was forever changed. Her vision and compassion paved the way for many people to die with grace. Her stages of death are stages many of us go through during our lives. Twenty two years ago she shaped my view of the death and dying experience. I'm humbled to include a small part of her work. When I began writing **"Into the Light"** I had no idea that I would be writing anything about Elisabeth Kubler Ross. Although her book *"On Death and Dying"* helped shape my view on death I never read any of her other books. I always said she was on my bucket list of people I wanted to meet. After I was finished writing Into the Light I did a web search about Elisabeth's life. I had no idea of the struggles she went through during her life. I found out she believed in an afterlife. This belief in the afterlife made it possible for people to ridicule her and try and discount her work with those dying. She made it possible for others to experience death with grace.

AUTHOR'S NOTES

I believe humankind is ready for another shift in consciousness. Comfort care and compassionate care of the dying must include care of the soul. Denying there is an afterlife and a place many call heaven keeps one trapped in physical consciousness. Expanding one's consciousness to embrace that within Creator God there are many planes of consciousness allows us to embrace heaven. In 1969 Elisabeth opened the doors for a shift in consciousness for the care of the dying.

In 2014 I believe *"Into the Light"* and *"Birthing Into Spirit"* will open doors for another shift in consciousness, one which will open the doors for birthing into spirit. A consciousness shift occurs within humanity when the masses embrace a new idea or concept. I believe humankind is ready to embrace that we are spiritual beings. By embracing that we are spiritual beings the doors will open up and we will walk into the light together. As humankind embraces the magnificence of the journey of our souls, we will embrace that yes, there is more, much more, to life and to physical death than we experience.

Information:

For information about Birthing Into Spirit Conferences and events go to: *www.KatyeAnna.com*

Want to be a host for a Birthing Into Spirit Conference and Event? Contact Katye Anna at *Chooselove@katyeanna.com*

For those who want more information about Elisabeth Kubler Ross go to: http://www.ekrfoundation.org/

Join KatyeAnna on FaceBook at: *https://www.facebook.com/ KatyeAnna*

ABOUT THE AUTHOR

Katye Anna has been teaching and transforming lives by sharing the teachings of her soul. Katye Anna lives a life infused with soul love. For more than twenty years, she has inspired and encouraged people to embrace the magnificence of who they are, incarnated souls.

Katye Anna shares information and insights that will inspire and challenge you to expand your consciousness. She is an inspirational speaker, teacher and author. Katye Anna and her husband Allan currently live in Pennsylvania.

If you enjoyed this book, we would appreciate it if you would post a positive review. Positive reviews help us reach more people with our message of hope. To post a review, all you need to do is go to the review section of this book's Amazon page. Click the button that says, "Write a customer review."

Thank you for your support.

Made in the USA
Middletown, DE
04 July 2019